REGENTS RENAISSANCE DRAMA SERIES

General Editor: **Cyrus Hoy**
Advisory Editor: **G. E. Bentley**

NO WIT, NO HELP LIKE A WOMAN'S

THOMAS MIDDLETON

No Wit, No Help
Like a Woman's

Edited by

LOWELL E. JOHNSON

UNIVERSITY OF NEBRASKA PRESS • LINCOLN

Library of Congress Cataloging in Publication Data

Middleton, Thomas, 1580?–1627.
    No wit, no help like a woman's.

    (Regents Renaissance drama series)
    Includes bibliographical references.
    I. Johnson, Lowell E., 1930. Ed.
        II. Title.
PR2714.M7 1976   822′.3   74-33673
ISBN 0–8032–0300–4

Regents Renaissance Drama Series

The purpose of the Regents Renaissance Drama Series is to provide soundly edited texts, in modern spelling, of the more significant plays of the Elizabethan, Jacobean, and Caroline theater. Each text in the series is based on a fresh collation of all sixteenth- and seventeenth-century editions. The textual notes, which appear above the line at the bottom of each page, record all substantive departures from the edition used as the copy-text. Variant substantive readings among sixteenth- and seventeenth-century editions are listed there as well. In cases where two or more of the old editions present widely divergent readings, a list of substantive variants in editions through the seventeenth century is given in an appendix. Editions after 1700 are referred to in the textual notes only when an emendation originating in some one of them is received into the text. Variants of accidentals (spelling, punctuation, capitalization) are not recorded in the notes. Contracted forms of characters' names are silently expanded in speech prefixes and stage directions, and, in the case of speech prefixes, are regularized. Additions to the stage directions of the copy-text are enclosed in brackets. Stage directions such as "within" or "aside" are enclosed in parentheses when they occur in the copy-text.

Spelling has been modernized along consciously conservative lines. "Murther" has become "murder," and "burthen," "burden," but within the limits of a modernized text, and with the following exceptions, the linguistic quality of the original has been carefully preserved. The variety of contracted forms ('em, 'am, 'm, 'um, 'hem) used in the drama of the period for the pronoun *them* are here regularly given as 'em, and the alternation between *a'th'* and *o'th'* (for *on* or *of the*) is regularly reproduced as *o'th'*. The copy-text distinction between preterite endings in -d and -ed is preserved except where the elision of e occurs in the penultimate syllable; in such cases, the final syllable is contracted. Thus, where the old editions read "threat'ned," those of the present series read "threaten'd." Where, in the old editions, a contracted preterite in -*y'd* would yield -*i'd* in modern spelling (as in "try'd," "cry'd," "deny'd"), the word is here given its full form (e.g. "tried," "cried," "denied").

Punctuation has been brought into accord with modern practices. The effort here has been to achieve a balance between the generally light pointing of the old editions, and a system of punctuation which, without overloading the text with exclamation marks, semicolons, and dashes, will make the often loosely flowing verse (and prose) of the original syntactically intelligible to the modern reader. Dashes are regularly used only to indicate interrupted speeches, or shifts of address within a single speech.

Explanatory notes, chiefly concerned with glossing obsolete words and phrases, are printed below the textual notes at the bottom of each page. References to stage directions in the notes follow the admirable system of the Revels editions, whereby stage directions are keyed, decimally, to the line of the text before or after which they occur. Thus, a note on 0.2 has reference to the second line of the stage direction at the beginning of the scene in question. A note on 115.1 has reference to the first line of the stage direction following line 115 of the text of the relevant scene.

CYRUS HOY

University of Rochester

Contents

Contents

List of Abbreviations

Bosanquet — E. F. Bosanquet. *English Printed Almanacks and Prognostications.* London, 1917.

Brand — John Brand. *Observations on Popular Antiquities.* London, 1900.

Brooke — Iris Brooke. *English Costume in the Age of Elizabeth.* London, 1938.

Bullen — A. H. Bullen, ed. *The Works of Thomas Middleton.* 8 vols. London, 1885–1886.

Copeman — W. S. C. Copeman. *Doctors and Disease in Tudor Times.* London, 1960.

Cotton — Charles Cotton. *The Compleat Gamester.* London, 1674.

DNB — *Dictionary of National Biography.*

Dyce — Alexander Dyce, ed. *The Works of Thomas Middleton.* 5 vols. London, 1840.

Lilly, *Christian Astrology* — William Lilly. *Christian Astrology.* London, 1647.

Lilly, *Introduction* — William Lilly. *An Introduction to Astrology,* ed. Zadkiel. London, 1852.

O — Octavo of 1657.

OED — *Oxford English Dictionary.*

Puttenham — George Puttenham. *The Arte of English Poesie.* London, 1589.

S.D. — Stage direction.

S.P. — Speech prefix.

Sugden — Edward H. Sugden. *A Topographical Dictionary to the Works of Shakespeare and His Fellow Dramatists.* Manchester, 1925.

Introduction

DATING AND AUTHORSHIP

The date of composition for *No Wit, No Help Like a Woman's* has been conjectural. Its date of publication, 1657, is of no value in this respect and there are no external references to the play's performance nor any contemporary mention of the play. The fact that the published version represents a 1638 revival further complicates the problem. Dating must come from internal evidence.

A. H. Bullen, the first critic who tried to determine the date of composition, argued for the period 1613–14 on the basis of Weatherwise's comment in III.i.279–82:

> If I that have proceeded in five and twenty such books of astronomy should not be able to put down a scholar now in one thousand six hundred thirty and eight, the dominical letter being G, I stood for a goose.

Recognizing that 1638 was only an updating by James Shirley in his revival of the play, Bullen simply subtracted the twenty-five books of astronomy (almanacs) from 1638 to derive the date 1613.[1] Frederick Fleay tried to reinforce that date by pointing out that the play takes place on Friday, 11 June (I.i.267), and that in 1613, 11 June did fall on a Friday.[2] One easily concurs with E. K. Chambers' comment on the dating procedures: "I feel no confidence in the argument."[3] Middleton scholars have continued to assign dates for *No Wit, No Help* ranging from 1610 until Middleton's death in 1627.

The play can be more accurately dated.[4] Weatherwise, the

1. A. H. Bullen, ed., *Works of Thomas Middleton* (London, 1885), 1:xl.

2. Frederick G. Fleay, *A Biographical Chronicle of the English Drama, 1559–1642* (London, 1891), 2:96.

3. E. K. Chambers, *The Elizabethan Stage* (Oxford, 1923), 3:441.

4. See my Ph.D. dissertation, "A Critical Edition of Thomas Middleton's *No Wit, No Help Like a Woman's*," (University of Wisconsin,

astrological fool, quotes several proverbs from the almanac which he continually consults (I.i.258 ff.; III.i.103 ff.; V.i.382; Epilogue). Such proverbs or catch-phrases were frequently printed in Renaissance almanacs, but Pond's Almanac, the only one mentioned by name in the play (III.i.97), did not print proverbs. Middleton certainly must have used Thomas Bretnor's 1611 almanac, in which fifteen of Weatherwise's sixteen catch-phrases occur.[5] Although Bretnor scatters the same catch-phrases in his later almanacs, the fifteen cited proverbs do appear together in 1611.[6]

It seems unlikely that an almanac would be consulted long after it was current: when Middleton used eleven proverbs in the *Inner Temple Masque* (performed at Christmas 1618 and published in 1619), he chose them from the 1618 Bretnor. There seems little doubt, therefore, that the date of composition for *No Wit, No Help* was 1611—probably the summer or early fall, judging by the many references in the play to the summer months.[7]

The authorship of the play is not a problem. Thomas Middleton is given full credit on the title page of the first edition, 1657, and every Middleton scholar has accepted the play as part of the canon on the basis of subject matter, treatment of theme, parallel passages, and linguistic evidence. Tentative suggestions at the end of the nineteenth century that William Rowley deserved some credit as a collaborator were proved foundationless and are now completely discredited.

1963), pp. lxxi–lxxvii, and David George, "Weather-wise's Almanac and the Date of Middleton's *No Wit, No Help Like a Woman's,*" *Notes and Queries* 211 (August 1966): 297–301.

5. In the single exception, Middleton altered "prittily preuented" of the original to "privily prevented" (III.i.110) for the sake of Pickadille's joke on a privy.

6. John Crow, "Some Jacobean Catch-Phrases and Some Light on Thomas Bretnor," *Elizabethan and Jacobean Studies* (Oxford, 1959), pp. 250–78.

7. Additional support for 1611 as the date of composition comes from the poesies quoted on the trencher plates in Weatherwise's banquet (II.i.62–73). These poesies are almost identical to those verses listed for the same months—May, June, and September—in Jeffery Neve's *Prognostication* for 1611. Neve does, however, repeat the rhymes for the same months in his almanacs of later years.

Middleton's text was only slightly revised for the 1638 revival of the play and that revised version served as printer's copy. Bullen was the first to state that the reviser was James Shirley, drawing his conclusion from Alexander Dyce's discovery that Shirley, while in Dublin from 1636 to 1640,[8] had written a prologue to a play called *No Wit to a Woman's*.[9] This prologue was not published in the 1657 edition of the play.[10] The only discernible revision of Shirley's which remains in Middleton's play is the updating of Weatherwise's reference to the current year at III.i.281.[11]

SOURCES

The classical nature of the subplot involving the Twilights and the Sunsets in *No Wit, No Help* is readily apparent, and naturally led nineteenth- and twentieth-century English and American critics to speculate on the Latin plays which might have served as its source. All of these scholars, with the exception of J. E. Spingarn,[12] were unaware of the identification by A. L. Stiefel in 1891 of the source of the Twilight-Sunset plot as Giambattista Della Porta's late sixteenth-century prose comedy, *La Sorella*.[13] That information passed almost unnoticed until the rediscovery of the relationship between the two works by D. J. Gordon in 1941. Gordon's extensive analysis of the two plays argues persuasively that Middleton was dependent upon Della Porta.[14]

8. Shirley evidently went to Ireland when the London theaters were closed in 1636 because of the plague.

9. Bullen, *Works*, 1:xl.

10. The prologue is included in *Dramatic Works and Poems of James Shirley*, ed. William Gifford and Alexander Dyce (London, 1833), 6:492–93.

11. Fleay made an argument for more extensive revision by Shirley, but neither of his proofs is supportable: one is too hypothetical, the other is erroneous.

12. J. E. Spingarn, ed., *Critical Essays of the Seventeenth Century* (Oxford, 1908), 2:335.

13. A. L. Stiefel, "Unbekannte italienische Quellen Jean de Rotrou's," *Zeitschrift für frazösische Sprache und Literatur*, Supp. 5 (1891), pp. 44–46.

14. D. J. Gordon, "Middleton's *No Wit, No Help Like a Woman's* and Della Porta's *La Sorella*," *Review of English Studies* 17 (1941): 400–414.

The existence of an English school play in Latin called *Adelphe* raises the possibility that Middleton may have consulted that play as an intermediate source. *Adelphe* was adapted from *La Sorella* by Samuel Brooke, Chaplain and later Master of Trinity College, Cambridge, for performance by his students.[15] A comparison of presentation of scenes, parallels in language, and treatment of themes in the three plays reveals that *Adelphe* was not Middleton's source;[16] it seems possible, rather, that Brooke may have been inspired by a performance of *No Wit, No Help* to turn to Della Porta. If so, the date 1611 for *No Wit, No Help* is reinforced, for the manuscript of Brooke's play records its first performance as 1611.[17]

Middleton saw in *La Sorella* a satisfactory plot complete with the traditional classical intrigues which made good stage fare; therefore he retained the general outline with most of its conventionality.[18] He did make a number of changes to bring the play into line with the successful city comedies he had been writing during the previous ten years. He set the locale in London, using English-born and London-bred characters and scenes to concentrate on the intrigues swirling around one of the two love affairs in *La Sorella*.[19] However, his adaptation is more than just compression. He altered the theme from a moral lesson

15. Samuel Brooke, "Adelphe," in MS. R.3.9, Trinity College Library, Cambridge University. For the Italian play, see Giambattista Della Porta, *La Sorella*, in *Le Commedie*, ed. Vincenzo Spampanato (Bari, 1910), 1:1–93.

16. For example, Middleton's II.ii.113 ff. is not in *Adelphe* but is in *La Sorella*; a Middleton passage at II.ii.32–33 is an echo of a metaphor used by Della Porta in the same scene but not found in *Adelphe*. Brooke also eliminates the sin of incest in his adaptation by keeping the young lovers unmarried and virtuous.

17. Stiefel's suggestion that Rotrou's *La Soeur* may have served as an intermediary source is clearly erroneous: Stiefel assumes that Rotrou's play (1645) predates Middleton's.

18 David Orr believes that *No Wit, No Help* "represents the last English comedy before the death of James I [1625] to be significantly indebted to Italian comedy" (*Italian Renaissance Drama in England Before 1625* [Chapel Hill, 1970], p 52).

19. Daniel C. Boughner, "Traditional Elements in Falstaff," *Journal of English and Germanic Philology* 43 (1944): 417–28, believes that Captain Trasimaco, the braggart warrior, one of the characters eliminated by Middleton, was probably "the repository of comic devices" from which Shakespeare drew the character of Falstaff.

showing good coming from evil to a presentation of woman's ingenuity and importance; he lessened the *commedia erudita* in favor of comedy of humors; and he transformed the prose into verse. On the whole, Middleton's adaptation is more interesting than its source.

There is a similarity between Weatherwise's banquet (II.i) and Trimalchio's banquet in the *Satyricon* by Petronius:[20] both are based on the twelve signs of the zodiac. If Middleton is indebted to the *Satyricon*, he improved on the original by assigning the guests to their appropriate signs (rather than the dishes to the signs, as did Trimalchio), thereby gaining an even more comic effect.

THE PLAY

The failure of *No Wit, No Help* to be produced in the past three hundred years is damning. Few of Middleton's plays escaped this judgment from the box office, until his resurrection by nineteenth-century critics. Even today, critical opinion on *No Wit, No Help* varies widely. Middleton's first editor, Alexander Dyce, considered the play one of the better comedies, recommending it along with Middleton's best known comedies. Charles Lamb chose six passages from the play to include in his *Specimens of English Dramatic Poets*, illustrating "what may be called the moral sense of our ancestors." A. H. Bullen termed the play "one of Middleton's ablest comedies"; A. G. Swinburne praised its "energetic invention and beautiful versification," saying it had "the unfailing charm of a style worthy of Fletcher himself."[21] On the other hand, some twentieth-century critics have not been as gentle or as complimentary. Richard Barker and Samuel Schoenbaum both find much to criticize in the play, although neither is willing to dismiss it entirely. Barker condemns the play as "a potboiler, an exercise in the fashionable manner of

20. The similarity was first noticed by F. Holthausen, "Zu Middleton's *No Wit, No Help Like a Woman's*," *Anglia* 12 (1889): 526–27.

21. Alexander Dyce, ed., *The Works of Thomas Middleton* (London, 1840), 1:1vi; Charles Lamb, *Specimens*, New Edition (London, 1854), pp. 141–43 and p. iv; Bullen, *Works*, 1:xl–xlii; introduction by A. G. Swinburne to *Thomas Middleton* in *Mermaid Series* (London, 1887–1890), 1:xix–xx.

Beaumont and Fletcher," says that it is "an unpretentious collection of farcical and melodramatic scenes," but grants that it does achieve a measure of success.[22] Schoenbaum believes that the play succeeds on its "own limited terms, but lack[s] the vitality, concreteness, and depth of social implication of Middleton's previous comedies."[23]

Undoubtedly the chief weakness of the play is its plot or plots. By 1611, the Renaissance comic plot of intrigue had become commonplace, and Middleton added no freshness or originality to the stereotypes. He combines two plot conventions, of the witty servant and of a woman in disguise, and links the two by many devices: Weatherwise begins as a suitor for Grace, but then becomes a suitor for Lady Goldenfleece; Jane is a cousin of Mrs. Low-water; the Widow knows a secret about Grace and Jane; all the characters know each other, in fact, all are gathered at Lady Goldenfleece's house at the end of the play. Each plot illustrates the title of the play which is also its thesis: Mrs. Low-water confounds her enemies, and succeeds in marrying her scholarly brother to the wealthy Lady Goldenfleece; Philip's mother extricates him from his difficulties with his father; and Lady Goldenfleece removes the sin of incest by revealing her secret. Middleton's plots are invariably the weakest part of his comedies; *A Chaste Maid in Cheapside,* sometimes considered his best comedy, has four plots. To judge the value of any Middleton comedy by its plot is to dismiss them all. What one remembers of Middleton's plays are scenes and characters.

Of the two plots, Middleton's own, of the Low-waters, is superior to the borrowed subplot because it exercises minimal constraint on the action and the characters. The emphasis in the Low-water scenes is not on the plot itself but on what emerges from it. The intrigues of the suitors result in their presenting a masque (IV.iii.40 ff.) which takes on dramatic significance beyond that of the plot itself. For instance, the intention of Sir Gilbert's speech (IV.iii.45–72) is to embarrass the widow by identifying her marriage with lust, but this serious accusation is tempered

22. Richard H. Barker, *Thomas Middleton* (New York, 1958), pp. 86–87.

23. Samuel Schoenbaum, "*A Chaste Maid in Cheapside* and Middleton's City Comedy," *Studies in the English Renaissance Drama* (New York, 1959), p. 308.

by reminiscences of a golden age, hence the audience reflects salaciously on one and dreamily on the other; plot complexities are secondary. The inserted masque also is as important for satisfying the audience's desire for spectacle, mixing entertainment with irony, as it is for plot resolution.[24]

Another memorable scene is Weatherwise's zodiacal banquet (II.i). The plot line is advanced by the scene when Sir Gilbert is dismissed in disgrace as a suitor for the widow, but its primary purpose is comic: Weatherwise is given an opportunity to display his humor in his elaborate conceit on the signs of the zodiac. Other scenes, such as the combat of wits between Weatherwise and Pickadille (III.i.76 ff.) and the questioning of the Dutch Boy by Savorwit (I.iii.114 ff.), indicate that even if Middleton could not concentrate his attentions enough to write an integrated plot, he was capable of delightful comic scenes.

Middleton's other achievements in the play are his characterizations, most notably Sir Oliver Twilight, Weatherwise, Mrs. Low-water, and Lady Goldenfleece. Each is endowed with a personality which expands on the basic convention. The characterization of Sir Oliver far exceeds his prototype, Pardo, in *La Sorella*, who is merely the stock figure of the miserly father. Sir Oliver has aspects of a humor character: it is his humor not to give a dowry to his daughter. Middleton raises him above buffoonery and derision by making him generous in spirit, compassionate, and friendly. Thus Sir Oliver's humor is offset by praiseworthy qualities which make him a pleasing character, one at whom the audience laughs, but who is treated respectfully, rather than satirically, by the dramatist.

Weatherwise's humor of living his life by the guidance of almanacs and astrology is his whole personality. Again, Middleton does not seek to flatten Weatherwise with heavy satire and ridicule; rather, he presents him as a merry gull. It is obvious from Middleton's handling of the astrological allusions that he is not sympathetic to astrologers; he considers astrology as ridiculous as the Lenten regulations which he satirized in *A Chaste Maid in Cheapside*. But astrology does allow for Middleton's characteristic taste for pseudo-learning.

24. Middleton undoubtedly was influenced by Beaumont and Fletcher's *The Maid's Tragedy* (1610) in using a wedding masque (I.ii) for ironic purposes.

The new date of *No Wit, No Help* raises the issue of the play as a transitional drama, bridging the periods of Middleton's city comedies of the first decade of the seventeenth century and that of his romances and tragicomedies of the second decade. *No Wit, No Help* has the ingredients of a city comedy: the wooing of a city widow, a lecherous knight, a witty servant, an avaricious businessman, a gulled young man, a practical merchantman, a husband duped by his wife, a son tricking his father, a London setting, a satirical tone, and an insight into city customs. Yet the satiric blow is softened by the Fletcherian romance influence, found on the English stage after 1609, particularly in Middleton's handling of Mrs. Low-water's disguise and in the shaping of the characters of the main plot.

The overriding atmosphere of *No Wit, No Help* is romantic. Middleton drifted with the new tide of Fletcherian romance in writing this play, endeavoring to combine his bent for comic realism with romance. The conjunction was not particularly successful, but Mrs. Low-water, the romantic heroine, is. She is patterned on the Fletcherian girl: witty, aggressive, disguised. Her husband is a pale figure, no more than a "following spirit"; it is she who regains their lost wealth by masquerading as a roaring boy, wooing the widow, and arranging the marriage of her brother, Beveril. Moreover, Middleton portions out the best lyrical passages to her (I.ii.1–26 and II.iii.245–62). The first passage, a soliloquy in which Mrs. Low-water appeals to her intellect as an escape from her predicament, is as good poetry as Middleton could write, combining lyricism with his usual incisive analysis. Mrs. Low-water is the first woman Middleton uses as the central figure in a play. She is unquestionably the dominant character in the main plot and is responsible for establishing the mood of the play. Although she assumes her disguise early in the play and functions mainly as a young man, the audience is never unaware that she is a woman.

Lady Goldenfleece, the widow, differs markedly from those widows that Middleton portrays in his city comedies. A London widow, like Widow Medler in *A Trick to Catch the Old One*, is a marketable commodity to be sold to the highest bidder regardless of the buyer's qualities or age; her wealth is her chief asset, sex her main interest, and, like Mistress Thomasine in *Michaelmas*

Term, she remarries quickly. In Middleton's earlier plays, respectable women play very minor roles; he is much more interested in the courtesan, the unfaithful wife, the roaring girl, the bawdy mother, the hypocritical Puritan gossip, and the conniving daughter. The widows in his city comedies are formed in the same mold; hence the wooing of a widow is an exercise in skulduggery. But the widow in *No Wit, No Help* is an honest woman who is regarded generally with admiration. This does not mean that her wooing is free of intrigue or is on a high moral level, but the fault is not hers. She even chastises the suitors for their sexually suggestive language and imagery (II.i.74–82) and is sympathetic to the foolish Weatherwise. Mrs. Low-water, Lady Goldenfleece's enemy, respects her enough to be enraged by Sir Gilbert's churlish designs on her. It is true that Lady Goldenfleece begins by selecting her husband for social, economic, and sexual reasons, much like Middleton's widows in his earlier comedies, but her final choice for a husband is based on love alone.

Middleton's vaunted psychological insight into women is not evident in his characterization of Lady Goldenfleece. The rapidity of her shifting desires foreshadows Beatrice-Joanna of *The Changeling*, but these vacillations are considered romantic vicissitudes, not tragic, nor moral, weaknesses. She even admonishes herself for her fickleness in love:

> Fly from my heart all variable thoughts.
> She that's entic'd by every pleasing object
> Shall find small pleasure, and as little rest.
> (II.i.268–70)

This sentiment is in keeping with the romances, not the city comedies, nor the tragedies.

Middleton's portrayals of Lady Goldenfleece and Mrs. Low-water are experiments for him; evidently he did not consider them unsuccessful, for women play increasingly more important roles in his later plays, and, after one rather bizarre attempt at a retro-disguise in *The Widow*, his heroines cast off men's clothes and become more feminine in appearance and behavior as Middleton's fascination with feminine psychology broadens and deepens. The path from Mrs. Low-water and Lady Goldenfleece leads to Beatrice-Joanna and Livia.

No Wit, No Help Like a Woman's is not one of Middleton's best comedies, but none of his romances and tragicomedies is. Middleton's comic vision lay in piercing hypocrisy and foibles with satire, in dramatizing manners, in realistic depictions of everyday city life—in other words, with his early comedies. In *No Wit, No Help*, one has the sense that Middleton was unsure of his purpose. The play is an experiment in a new form, but Middleton was not confident enough to develop Fletcher's conventions, nor willing to give up the techniques of his successful city comedies. He seems to be satisfied, too often in the play, to exploit a type, to present a conventional intrigue, to rely on stage tricks, and to accept a new dramatic genre without adapting it to his own comic vision. For instance, his treatment of incest in the play lacks clarity of intention. He is not interested in the consequences of this sexual transgression (a theme he would not pass up in his tragedies), but in the manifestations of the sin. Yet the manifestations are washed aside by the device of a death-bed secret.

There is no record of any production of *No Wit, No Help* after 1638; nevertheless the play has been honored by imitation, if not presentation. In London, 1677, *The Counterfeit Bridegroom: or the Defeated Widow*, by either Aphra Behn or Thomas Betterton, was published. It is a fairly close adaptation of *No Wit, No Help*, retaining both plots and the basic intrigue, yet altering them to present a Restoration comedy of manners. Beveril is transformed into Mr. Noble, a man of mode; the Widow becomes a typical Restoration lady of liaisons; Sir Oliver is greedier; Sandfield becomes Mr. Sanders, supposedly a rich eunuch (influence of *The Country Wife?*); the Low-waters are renamed, appropriately, the Hadlands. There is much talk of extramarital love, sex is a preoccupation, the comic scenes are more farcical, and bawdy talk and drinking dominate. But the general outline of Middleton's play is followed, including the masque and Weatherwise's zodiacal banquet; indeed, one stage direction refers to "Mrs. Low[-water]" rather than "Mrs. Hadland."

A succession of adaptations of *The Counterfeit Bridegroom* followed over the next century. William Taverner's *The Artful Husband*, first acted in 1717, retained the Low-water plot from

Middleton's play as it was revised for *The Counterfeit Bride-groom*. Taverner's play was later revised by George Colman the Elder as *Female Chevalier* (1778), which in turn was the source of Alicia Sheridan's *Ambiguous Lover* (1781) and William Mac-ready's *The Bank Note, or Lesson for Ladies* (1795).[25] All these plays retained the Low-water plot from *No Wit, No Help*, an indication of the continued appreciation audiences had for Mid-dleton's own plot as opposed to the one he borrowed from *La Sorella*.

THE TEXT

One of the many plays that Humphrey Moseley entered in the Stationers' Register on 9 September 1653 was "No Witt, No Helpe, Like a Woman" by "Tho. Midleton."[26] Three years later, Moseley published a twenty-page advertisement of books for sale; the last title of the 246 listed is described as a book "I do purpose to Print very speedtly": "No Witt/ Help Like a Womans." The following year, 1657, the play was published, thirty years after the death of Thomas Middleton and prob-ably forty-six years after its composition. Its title page reads: "No { Wit / Help } Like/ A/ Womans./ A/ Comedy,/ By/ Tho. Middleton, Gent./ [Ornament]/ London:/ Printed for Humphrey Moseley, at the/ Prince's Arms in St. Pauls Church-/ yard. 1657." This edition, an octavo, was the only publication of the play until the nineteenth century.

Thomas Newcomb was the printer that Moseley employed for the publication, for the two ornaments used in the printing, one on the title page and the other a decorative initial appear-ing in the first word of the text, belonged to Newcomb.[27] Two other Middleton plays printed in 1657 by Newcomb for Moseley were *More Dissemblers Besides Women* and *Women Beware Women*. Each play was issued with its own title page, but these

---

25. John Genest, *Some Account of the English Stage* (Bath, 1832), 1:213; 2:609; 6:30–31; 7:214. I used the Huntington Library copies of *The Counterfeit Bridegroom* and *The Artful Husband* for comparisons.

26. W. W. Greg, *A Bibliography of the English Printed Drama to the Restoration* (London, 1951), 2:886, no. 778.

27. C. William Miller, "Thomas Newcomb: A Restoration Printer's Ornament Stock," *Studies in Bibliography* 3 (1950), insert facing p. 160.

last two were also bound together under a separate title page, *Two New Playes*. Some copies of *No Wit, No Help* evidently were bound with these two plays, for Gerard Langbaine, in 1691, wrote that the three plays "are all in one Volume."[28] The only bibliographic difficulty presented by the close association of these three is the pedigree of an engraved portrait of Middleton, crowned with laurels, and inscribed "Vera Effiges/ Tho: Middletoni Gent:." This engraving precedes the initial gathering in some copies of *Two New Playes* and appears in some single copies of *No Wit, No Help*. W. W. Greg contends that the portrait belongs to the *Two New Playes*, but acknowledges that the two copies of *No Wit, No Help* that he inspected which have the portrait are "still in the original sheep, which suggests that the addition may have been made at the time of publication."[29] The portrait probably was a job-lot printing to enhance the sales of as many volumes of Middleton's plays as possible.

Nineteen copies of the 1657 octavo of *No Wit, No Help* are known to exist, an unusually large number of a seventeenth-century play.[30] Six of these copies were examined and collated for this edition: octavos now found at the Bodleian, the Huntington, the Folger, the Newberry, the University of Chicago, and Harvard. The Folger and the Huntington copies have the portrait of Middleton; the Newberry and the Huntington copies have the twenty-page advertisement bound up with the text; and the Bodleian, the Chicago, and the Harvard copies have neither addition. The octavo is collated: A1, title page; A1v, blank; A2, prologue; A2v, actors' names; A3–H3, text; H3v, epilogue; H4, blank. Page 30 is misprinted as 32, page 83 as 77, indicating that the printers used catch-words and signatures, not pagination, in assembling the pages.

The 1657 octavo is well printed by seventeenth-century standards. It has few serious cruxes; inking and general legibility are good. The text is liberally sprinkled with broken colons which were used in place of periods. Heavy punctuation, characteristic

28. Gerard Langbaine, *An Account of the English Dramatick Poets* (Oxford, 1691), p. 374.

29. Greg, *Bibliography*, 2:886.

30. A consensus figure from Greg's *Bibliography*, 2:886, and Gertrude L. Woodward and James G. McManaway's *Check List of English Plays 1641–1700* (Chicago, 1945), entry no. 815.

of seventeenth-century dramatic texts, was employed, causing some difficulties in making a modern English edition, but the most problematical area is the confusion between prose and verse in the octavo. (Every instance in which the present edition changes verse lines to prose or vice versa has been recorded in the textual notes.) The octavo is divided into acts, but not scenes, a procedure characteristic of Middleton. The act divisions are conventional, not structural: the first two acts comprise over half the play; the third act is extremely short.

There is ample evidence that two compositors, working seriatim, set the octavo, and that the change in compositors occurred between gatherings C and E. The second compositor was in general more space-conscious than the first. He used more contractions, set the only thirty-seven-line page (H1v) in the text (the rest are thirty-six lines), and was satisfied to use only "I" for a catchword rather than "I can" or "I assure" as the first compositor did. Moreover, the second compositor used shorter speech prefixes: "Sir Ol." rather than "Sir Oliv." for example. Another difference between them is in the speech prefix for Sir Gilbert Lambston. It is always "Lambst." until his exit in gathering C8, but when he returns, at gathering E2, it becomes "Sir Gilb." Finally, the peculiarity of ending speeches with commas or semicolons instead of periods occurs almost entirely after the C gathering.

There is no evidence that Newcomb used two presses in printing the octavo, nor that the compositors "cast-off" copy. The collation of six copies indicated that few if any proofreading corrections were made after the printing of a forme commenced. The few variants appear to be type-face deterioration over the course of a press-run, or inking and paper flaws.

The manuscript which the printer used as his copy-text was probably not a holograph of Middleton, nor a prompt book. The printed text lacks many of the idiosyncrasies of Middleton's handwriting and does not contain the carefully edited stage directions one assumes would be found in a prompt book. The printer's copy was, more than likely, either the work of a professional scribe who followed Middleton's foul papers quite faithfully and on which Shirley made his change of date, or else the work of a scribe who carefully recopied Middleton's foul papers in the mid-1630s for Shirley's use.

The only published editions of *No Wit, No Help* after the 1657 octavo and before this present edition are two published in the nineteenth century: one by Alexander Dyce in volume five of his *Works of Thomas Middleton* (1840), and the other by A. H. Bullen in volume four of his *Works of Thomas Middleton* (1885). Every Middleton editor is conscious of Dyce's excellent work in solving cruxes, identifying verse passages, and providing explanatory notes. Though Bullen's edition is little more than a reprinting of Dyce's, he did contribute some important explanatory notes, and his introduction, though dated, is of value. I trust this present edition of *No Wit, No Help Like a Woman's* would satisfy Thomas Middleton's request in his epistle "To the Reader" prefixed to his *Father Hubburd's Tales:* "I never wished this book better fortune than to fall into the hands of a true-spelling printer, and an honest-minded bookseller."[31] In addition to the usual acknowledgment to family, friends, and teachers, I wish to give particular thanks to Saint Olaf College and to the American Lutheran Church for research grants.

LOWELL E. JOHNSON

Saint Olaf College

31. Dyce, ed., *Works*, 5:553.

NO WIT, NO HELP LIKE A WOMAN'S

THE ACTORS' NAMES

SIR OLIVER TWILIGHT, *a rich old knight*
PHILIP, *his son, servant to Mistress Grace*
SANDFIELD, *friend to Philip, servant to Mistress Jane*
MASTER SUNSET, *true father of Mistress Grace*
MASTER LOW-WATER, *a decayed gentleman*   5
SIR GILBERT LAMBSTON ⎫
MASTER WEATHERWISE   ⎪
MASTER PEPPERTON   ⎬ *suitors to the Lady Goldenfleece*
MASTER OVERDON   ⎭   10
MASTER BEVERIL, *brother to Mistress Low-water*
DUTCH MERCHANT
DUTCH BOY
SAVORWIT, *Sir Oliver's man*
FOOTMAN   15
PICKADILLE, *Lady Goldenfleece's fool*
LADY TWILIGHT
LADY GOLDENFLEECE, *a rich widow*
MISTRESS LOW-WATER
MISTRESS GRACE, *Sunset's daughter, but supposed Twilight's*   20
MISTRESS JANE, *Twilight's daughter, but supposed Sunset's*

The Scene, *London*

---

2. *servant*] suitor.
5. *decayed*] impoverished.
6. *Lambston*] i.e., "lamb stone" or lamb's testicles, implying lechery. Middleton frequently used tag names, hence the "wit" in the name of the witty servant, Savorwit, and the sexual exhaustion of Overdon, who is past fifty. Both Sir Oliver Twilight and Master Sunset are in the evenings of their lives; Weatherwise is a devotee of almanacs; Lady Goldenfleece is a rich widow. The name Low-water suggests impoverishment; and the name of the clown, Pickadille, suggests the analogy between a pickadille (an intricate, delicate edging on a collar) and the intricate schemes in the plot for which the clown is responsible.

PROLOGUE

How is't possible to suffice
So many ears, so many eyes?
Some in wit, some in shows
Take delight, and some in clothes;
Some for mirth they chiefly come,   5
Some for passion—for both some;
Some for lascivious meetings, that's their arrant;
Some to detract, and ignorance their warrant.
How is't possible to please
Opinion toss'd in such wild seas?   10
Yet I doubt not, if attention
Seize you above, and apprehension
You below, to take things quickly,
We shall both make you sad and tickle ye.

---

7. *arrant*] variant of errand, needed for the rhyme.

No Wit, No Help Like a Woman's

Enter Philip, *Sir Oliver Twilight's son, with* Savorwit, *his father's man.*

PHILIP,
    I am at my wit's ends, Savorwit.
SAVORWIT.
    And I am ev'n following after you as fast as I can, sir.
PHILIP.
    My wife will be forc'd from me, my pleasure!
SAVORWIT,
    Talk no more on't, sir. How can there be any
    Hope i'th' middle when we're both at our   5
    Wit's end in the beginning? My invention
    Was ne'er so gravel'd since I first set out upon't.
PHILIP.
    Nor does my stop stick only in this wheel,
    Though it be a main vexation, but I'm grated
    In a dear absolute friend, young Master Sandfield—   10
SAVORWIT.
    Ay, there's another rub, too.
PHILIP.   —Who supposes
    That I make love to his affected mistress,
    When 'tis my father works against the peace
    Of both our spirits, and woos unknown to me.
    He strikes out sparks of undeserved anger,   15

4–7.] *this edn.; in* O *lines end* be/
wits/ gra-/ upon't.

---

7. *gravel'd*] perplexed.
9. *grated*] harassed.
12. *affected mistress*] woman whom he loves.

'Twixt old steel friendship, and new stony hate,
As much forgetful of the merry hours
The circuits of our youth hath spent and worn,
As if they had not been, or we not born.

SAVORWIT.

See where he comes.

Enter Sandfield.

SANDFIELD.   Unmerciful in torment!   20
Will this disease never forsake mine eye?

PHILIP.

It must be kill'd first, if it grow so painful.
Work it out strongly at one time that th'anguish
May never more come near thy precious sight.
If my eternal sleep will give thee rest,   25
Close up mine eyes with opening of my breast.

SANDFIELD.

I feel thy wrongs at midnight and the weight
Of thy close treacheries. Thou hast a friendship
As dangerous as a strumpet's, that will kiss
Men into poverty, distress, and ruin;   30
And to make clear the face of thy foul deeds,
Thou work'st by seconds.   [*Draws his sword.*]

PHILIP.

Then may the sharp point of an inward horror
Strike me to earth, and save thy weapon guiltless.

SANDFIELD.

Not in thy father?   35

PHILIP.

How much is truth abus'd when 'tis kept silent!

SANDFIELD.

Oh, defend me friendship!

SAVORWIT.

True, your anger's in an error all this while, sir;
But that a lover's weapon ne'er hears reason,
'Tis out still like a mad man's. Hear but me, sir.   40

37.SP. SANDFIELD] *Dyce;* PHILIP *O.*   39. ne'er] *Dyce;* now *O.*

40. *still*] always.

'Tis my young master's injury, not yours,
That you quarrel with him for, and this shows
As if y'would challenge a lame man the field
And cut off's head because he has lost his legs.
His grief makes him dead flesh, as it appear'd   45
By off'ring up his breast to you; for believe it, sir,
Had he not greater crosses of his own,
Your hilts could not cross him—

SANDFIELD.   How?
SAVORWIT.   Not your hilts, sir.
Come, I must have you friends; a pox of weapons!
There's a whore gapes for't; put it up i'th' scabbard.   50

SANDFIELD [*puts up his sword*].
Thou'rt a mad slave.
SAVORWIT.   Come, give me both your hands.
Y'are in a quagmire both; should I release you now,
Your wits would both come home in a stinking pickle;
Your father's old nose would smell you out presently.

PHILIP.
Tell him the secret, which no mortal knows   55
But thou and I, and then he will confess
How much he wrong'd the patience of his friend.

SAVORWIT.
Then thus the marigold opens at the splendor
Of a hot constant friendship 'twixt you both.
'Tis not unknown to your ear, some ten years since   60
My mistress, his good mother, with a daughter
About the age of six, crossing to Guernsey,
Was taken by the Dunkirks, sold both, and separated,
As the last news brings hot—the first and last
So much discover'd; for in nine years' space   65
No certain tidings of their life or death
Or what place held 'em, earth, the sea, or heaven,
Came to the old man's ears, the knight my master,
Till about five months since, a letter came,
Sent from the mother, which related all   70

54. mad] *Dyce;* made *O.*

---

63. *Dunkirks*] privateers from Dunkirk.

Their taking, selling, separation,
And never meeting; and withal required
Six hundred crowns for ransom, which my old master
No sooner heard the sound, but told the sum,
Gave him the gold, and sent us both aboard.   75
We landing by the way, having a care
To lighten us of our carriage because gold
Is such a heavy metal, eas'd our pockets
In wenches' aprons. Women were made to bear,
But for us gentlemen, 'tis most unkindly.   80

SANDFIELD.
Well, sir?

PHILIP.   A pure rogue still!

SAVORWIT.   Amongst the rest sir,
'Twas my young master's chance there to dote finely
Upon a sweet young gentlewoman, but one
That would not sell her honor for the Indies,
Till a priest struck the bargain, and then half a crown
    dispatch'd it.   85
To be brief, wedded her and bedded her,
Brought her home hither to his father's house,
And with a fair tale of mine own bringing up,
She passes for his sister that was sold.

SANDFIELD.
Let me not lost myself in wond'ring at thee.   90
But how made you your score even for the mother?

SAVORWIT.
Pish, easily; we told him how her fortunes
Mock'd us, as they mock'd her. When we were o'th' sea,
She was o'th' land, and as report was given,
When we were landed, she was gone to heaven.   95
So he believes two lies one error bred:
The daughter ransom'd and the mother dead.

SANDFIELD.
Let me admire thee and withal confess
My injuries to friendship.

---

74. *told*] counted out.
75. *him*] Philip.
80. *unkindly*] unnatural

PHILIP.   They're all pardon'd.   [*Embracing*.]
    These are the arms I bore against my friend.   100
SAVORWIT.
    But what's all this to th' present? This discourse
    Leaves you i'th' bog still.
PHILIP.   On, good Savorwit.
SAVORWIT,
    For yet our policy has cross'd ourselves;
    For the old knave, my master, little thinking her
    Wife to his son, but his own daughter still,   105
    Seeks out a match for her—
PHILIP.   Here I feel the surgeon
    At second dressing.
SAVORWIT.   —And h'as entertain'd
    Ev'n for pure need, for fear the glass should crack
    That is already broken, but well solder'd,
    A mere sot for her suitor, a rank fox,   110
    One Weatherwise, that woos by the almanac,
    Observes the full and change, an errant moon-calf.
    And yet, because the fool demands no portion
    But the bare down of her smock, the old fellow,
    Worn to the bone with a dry covetous itch,   115
    To save his purse and yet bestow his child,
    Consents to waste her on lumps of almanac stuff
    Kned with May-butter. —Now as I have thought on't
    I'll spoil him in the baking.
SANDFIELD.   Prithee, as how, sirrah?
SAVORWIT.
    I'll give him such a crack in one o'th' sides,   120
    He shall quite run out of my master's favor.
PHILIP,
    I should but too much love thee for that.
SAVORWIT.   Thus, then,
    To help you both at once, and so good night to you.

115. covetous] *Dyce;* courteous *O.*   117. her on] *Dyce; not in O.*

---

112. *moon-calf*] a born fool.
118. *Kned*] kneaded.
118. *May-butter*] unsalted butter used for medicinal purposes.

After my wit has shipp'd away the fool,
As he shall part, I'll buzz into the ear   125
Of my old master that you, sir, Master Sandfield,
Dearly affect his daughter and will take her
With little or no portion. Well stood out in't.
Methinks I see him caper at that news
And in the full cry, oh! This brought about   130
And wittily dissembled on both parts,
You to affect his love, he to love yours,
I'll so beguile the father at the marriage
That each shall have his own, and both being welcom'd
And chamber'd in one house, as 'tis his pride   135
To have his children's children got successively
On his forefathers' feather beds, in the day times,
To please the old man's eyesight, you may dally
And set a kiss on the wrong lip; no sin in't,
Brothers and sisters do't, cousins do more,   140
But pray take heed you be not kin to them.
So in the night time, nothing can deceive you,
Let each know his own work, and there I leave you.

SANDFIELD.
    Let me applaud thee.
PHILIP.   Bless'd be all thy ends
    That mak'st arm'd enemies embracing friends.   145
    About it speedily.   *Exit* [*with* Master Sandfield].
SAVORWIT.   I need no pricking.
    I'm of that mettle, so well pac'd and free,
    There's no good riders that use spur to me.

Enter Grace Twilight.

    Oh, are you come?
GRACE.   Are any comforts coming?
SAVORWIT.
    I never go without 'em.   150

148.1.] *S.D. in middle of l. 149 in
O.*

---

136. *got*] begot.
149. *comforts*] joys. Used as a double entendre in l. 158.

GRACE.

Thou sport'st joys that utterance cannot perfect.

SAVORWIT.

Hark, are they risen?

GRACE.   Yes, long before I left 'em.

And all intend to bring the widow homeward.

SAVORWIT.

Depart then, mistress, to avoid suspect.

Our good shall arrive time enough at your heart.   155

[*Exit* Grace.]

Poor fools that ever more take a green surfeit

Of the first fruits of joys. Let a man but shake the tree,

How soon they'll hold up their laps to receive comfort!

The music that I struck made her soul dance.—

Peace.

Enter the Lady Widow Goldenfleece *with* Sir Gilbert Lambston,
Master Pepperton, Master Overdon, *suitors. After them, the two
old men,* Sir Oliver Twilight *and* Master Sunset, *with their daughters,* Grace Twilight, [*and*] Jane Sunset.

[*Aside.*] Here comes the Lady Widow, the late wife 160

To the deceas'd Sir Avarice Goldenfleece,

Second to none for usury and extortion,

As too well it appears on a poor gentleman,

One Master Low-water, from whose estate

He pull'd that fleece that makes his widow weight.   165

Those are her suitors now, Sir Gilbert Lambston,

Master Pepperton, Master Overdon.

LADY GOLDENFLEECE.

Nay, good Sir Oliver Twilight, Master Sunset,

We'll trouble you no farther.

SUNSET. SIR OLIVER.   No trouble, sweet madam.

SIR GILBERT.

We'll see the widow at home; it shall be our charge that. 170

LADY GOLDENFLEECE.

It shall be so indeed.

Thanks, good Sir Oliver, and to you both

I am indebted for those courtesies
That will ask me a long time to requite.

SIR OLIVER.

Ah, 'tis but your pleasant condition to give it out so,
madam.   175

LADY GOLDENFLEECE.

Mistress Grace and Mistress Jane, I wish you both
A fair contented fortune in your choices,
And that you happen right.

GRACE. JANE.   Thanks to you, good madam.

LADY GOLDENFLEECE [aside].

There's more in that word "right" than you imagine.—
I now repent, girls, a rash oath I took   180
When you were both infants, to conceal a secret.

GRACE.

What does't concern, good madam?

LADY GOLDENFLEECE.   No, no.

Since you are both so well, 'tis well enough.
It must not be reveal'd; 'tis now no more
Than like mistaking of one hand for t'other.   185
A happy time to you both.

GRACE. JANE.   The like to you, madam.

GRACE [aside].

I shall long much to have this riddle open'd.

JANE [aside].

I would you were so kind to my poor kinswoman
And the distressed gentleman her husband,
Poor Master Low-water, who on ruin leans.   190
You keep this secret as you keep his means.

LADY GOLDENFLEECE.

Thanks, good Sir Oliver Twilight. Welcome, sweet
Master Pepperton; Master Overdon, welcome.

Exeunt. Manet Sir Oliver with Savorwit.

178, 186.S.P. GRACE. JANE] *Dyce;*
BOTH *O.*

179.S.P. LADY GOLDENFLEECE] *this*
edn.; BOTH *O;* GRACE *Dyce.*

192.S.P. LADY GOLDENFLEECE] *Dyce;*
JANE *O.*

192–3.] *this edn.; in O lines end*
Twilight,/ Pepperton,/ welcome.

---

179. S.P. *Lady Goldenfleece*] This line is assigned to the widow because she seems to be hinting at the secret.

SIR OLIVER.

    And, goes the business well 'twixt those young lovers?

SAVORWIT.

    Betwixt your son and Master Sunset's daughter,   195
    The line goes even, sir.

SIR OLIVER.   Good lad, I like thee.

SAVORWIT.

    But sir, there's no proportion, height, or evenness
    Betwixt that equinoctial and your daughter.

SIR OLIVER.

    'Tis true, and I'm right glad on't.

SAVORWIT.   Are you glad, sir?
    There's no proportion in't.

SIR OLIVER.   Ay, marry am I, sir.   200
    I can abide no word that ends in portion;
    I'll give her nothing.

SAVORWIT.   Say you should not, sir,
    As I'll ne'er urge your worship 'gainst your nature,
    Is there no gentleman, think you, of worth and credit
    Will open's bed to warm a naked maid?   205
    A hundred gallant fellows, and be glad
    To be so set awork. Virginity
    Is no such cheap ware as you make account on,
    That it had need with portion be set off,
    For that sets off a portion in these days.   210

SIR OLIVER.

    Play on, sweet boy!
    Oh, I could hear this music all day long,
    When there's no money to be parted from.
    Strike on, good lad!

SAVORWIT.

    Do not wise men and great often bestow   215
    Ten thousand pound in jewels that lie by 'em?
    If so, what jewel can lie by a man

211–14.] *Dyce; 2 lines in O, ending* long,/ **Lad.**

---

196. *The line goes even*] The matter is moving straight on.
198. *equinoctial*] celestial equator, referring to Weatherwise.

More precious than a virgin? If none more precious,
Why should the pillow of a fool be grac'd
With that brave spirits with dearness have embrac'd?   220
And then, perhaps, ere the third spring come on,
Sends home your diamond crack'd, the beauty gone;
And more to know her, 'cause you shall not doubt her,
A number of poor sparks twinkling about her.

SIR OLIVER.
Now thou play'st Dowland's *Lachrymae* to thy master.   225

SAVORWIT.
But shall I dry your eyes with a merry jig now
And make you look like sunshine in a shower?

SIR OLIVER.
How, how, my honest boy, sweet Savorwit?

SAVORWIT.
Young Master Sandfield, gallant Master Sandfield—

SIR OLIVER.
Ha! What of him?

SAVORWIT.   Affects your daughter strangely.   230

SIR OLIVER.
Brave Master Sandfield! —Let me hug thy zeal
Unto thy master's house. —Ha, Master Sandfield!
But he'll expect a portion!

SAVORWIT.   Not a whit, sir,
As you may use the matter.

SIR OLIVER.
Nay, and the matter fall into my using   235
The devil a penny that he gets of me.

SAVORWIT.
He lies at the mercy of your lock and key, sir;
You may use him as you list.

SIR OLIVER.   Say'st thou me so?
Is he so far in doing?

237–43.] *this edn.; in O lines end*
Key/ list./ do-/ ing?/ he/ some/
not./ Gri-/ 'em.

---

224. *sparks*] gallants, literally small diamonds.
225. *Dowland's* Lachrymae] John Dowland (1563?–1626?) published
his "celebrated '*Lachrymae,* or Seven Teares, figured in seaven pas-
sionate Pavans'" in 1605 *(DNB).*

SAVORWIT.   Quite over head and ears, sir.
  Nay more, he means to run mad and break his neck   240
  Off some high steeple, if he have her not.
SIR OLIVER.
  Now bless the young gentleman's gristles; I hope
  To be a grandfather yet by 'em.
SAVORWIT.   That may you sir,
  To, marry, a chopping girl with a plump buttock,
  Will hoist a farthingale at five years' old,   245
  And call a man between eleven and twelve
  To take part of a piece of mutton with her.
SIR OLIVER.
  Ha, precious wag! Hook him in finely, do.
SAVORWIT.
  Make clear the way for him first; set the gull going.
SIR OLIVER.
  An ass, an ass, I'll quickly dash his wooing.   250
SAVORWIT [aside].
  Why now the clocks
  Go right again. It must be a strange wit
  That makes the wheels of youth and age so hit;
  The one are dry, worn, rusty, fur'd, and soil'd;
  Love's wheels are glib, ever kept clean, and oil'd.   *Exit.* 255
SIR OLIVER.
  I cannot choose but think of this good fortune;
  That gallant Master Sandfield.

Enter Weatherwise.

WEATHERWISE [aside].   Stay, stay, stay!
  What comfort gives my almanac today?   [*Reads his almanac*]
  Luck, I beseech thee! "Good days," "evil days," "June,"
  "July"; speak a good word for me now, and I have her. 260

---

242. *gristles*] bones.
244. *chopping*] "a fine healthy, strong child" *(OED).*
245. *farthingale*] a woman's hooped skirt.
247. *a piece of mutton*] euphemism for love-making.
249. *gull*] fool.
254. *fur'd*] incrusted.
258. *my almanac*] See Introduction, p. xii.

—Let me see, "the fifth day, 'twixt hawk and buzzard;
the sixth day, backward and forward"—that was beastly
to me, I remember; "the seventh day, on a slippery pin;
the eighth day, fire and tow; the ninth day, the market is
marr'd"—that's long of the hucksters, I warrant you; but 265
now "the tenth day"—luck, I beseech thee now before I
look into't; "the eleventh day, against the hair"—a pox
on't! Would that hair had been left out—"against the
hair!" That hair will go nigh to choke me; had it been
against anything but that 'twould not have troubled me 270
because it lies cross i'th' way. Well, I'll try the fortune of
a good face yet, though my almanac leave me i'th' sands.

SIR OLIVER [aside].

Such a match, too. I could not wish a better.

WEATHERWISE [aside].

Mass, here he walks! —Save you, sweet Sir Oliver—Sir
Oliver Twilight!   275

SIR OLIVER.

Oh, pray come to me a quarter of a year hence; I have a
little business now.

WEATHERWISE.

How, a quarter of a year hence? What, shall I come to
you in September?

SIR OLIVER.

Nor in November neither, good my friend.   280

WEATHERWISE.

Y'are not a mad knight; you will not let your daughter
hang past August, will you? She'll drop down under tree,
then. She's no winter fruit, I assure you, if you think to
put her in crust after Christmas!

SIR OLIVER.

Sir, in a word, depart; my girl's not for you;   285
I gave you a drowsy promise in a dream,
But broad awake now, I call't in again.
Have me commended to your wit; farewell, sir.   [Exit.]

---

263. *pin*] peg.
264. *tow*] the flax on the distaff of a spinning wheel.
265. *that's . . . hucksters*] that's because of the grain speculators.
272. *leave . . . sands*] leave me in the lurch.

WEATHERWISE.

Now the devil run away with you, and some lousy fiddler
with your daughter. May Clerkenwell have the first cut 290
of her and Hound's Ditch pick the bones. I'll never
leave the love of an open-hearted widow for a narrow-
ey'd maid again; go out of the road way like an ass to
leap over hedge and ditch; I'll fall into the beaten path
again and invite the widow home to a banquet. Let who 295
list seek out new ways, I'll be at my journey's end before
him.
My almanac told me true, how I should fare;
Let no man think to speed against the hair.   *Exit.*

[I.ii]   *Enter* Mistress Low-water.

MISTRESS LOW-WATER.

Is there no saving-means? No help religious
For a distressed gentlewoman to live by?
Has virtue no revenue? Who has all then?
Is the world's lease from hell, the devil head-landlord?
Oh, how was conscience, the right heir, put by?   5
Law would not do such an unrighteous deed,
Though with the fall of angels 't had been fee'd.
Where are our hopes in banks? Was honesty
A younger sister without portion left?
No dowry in the Chamber beside wantonness?   10

I.ii.] *Dyce; no scene division in O.*   4. devil] *Dyce; Devils O.*

---

290. *Clerkenwell*] a district on the London north side; it had "a
particularly bad reputation as a haunt of thieves and loose women"
(Sugden).
291. *Hound's Ditch*] a London city street "mainly occupied by
brokers, i.e. old clothes dealers" (Sugden). Note pun on "hounds."
[I.ii]
3. *Has virtue no revenue?*] This phrase and others in the speech are
similar to those in *The Revenger's Tragedy*, II.i.1–8, a play often at-
tributed to Middleton.
10. *the Chamber*] the treasury of the City of London, in which
orphans' inheritances were deposited until they came of age. Middleton
and his sister, Avis, received their inheritance from the Chamber (see
Mark Eccles, " 'Thomas Midleton a Poett,' " *Studies in Philology* 54
[1957]: 517).

O miserable orphan!
'Twixt two extremes runs there no blessed mean,
No comfortable strain that I may kiss it?
Must I to whoredom, or to beggary lean,
My mind being sound? Is there no way to miss it?   15
Is't not injustice that a widow laughs
And lays her mourning part upon a wife?
That she should have the garment, I the heart;
My wealth her uncle left her, and me her grief?
Yet, stood all miseries in their loathed'st forms   20
On this hand of me, thick like a foul mist,
And here the bright enticements of the world
In clearest colors, flattery, and advancement,
And all the bastard glories this frame jets in,
Horror nor splendor, shadows fair nor foul   25
Should force me shame my husband, wound my soul.

         Enter Mistress Jane, *Sunset's daughter.*

Cousin, y'are welcome. This is kindly done of you
To visit the despis'd.
JANE.   I hope not so, coz.
The want of means cannot make you despis'd;
Love not by wealth but by desert is priz'd.   30
MISTRESS LOW-WATER.
Y'are pleas'd to help it well, coz.
JANE.   I am come to you,
Beside my visitation, to request you
To lay your wit to mine, which is but simple,
And help me to untie a few dark words
Made up in knots—they're of the widow's knitting,   35
That ties all sure—for my wit has not strength
Nor cunning to unloose 'em.
MISTRESS LOW-WATER.   Good, what are they?
Though there be little comfort of my help.

---

    13. *strain*] harmonious melody.
    19. *uncle*] should read "husband," but Middleton failed to change the relationship from the source play's "uncle."
    24. *this frame jets in*] this world struts in.

JANE.

    She wish'd Sir Oliver's daughter and myself
    Good fortune in our choices and repented her   40
    Of a rash oath she took when we were both infants,
    A secret to conceal; but since all's well,
    She holds it best to keep it unreveal'd.
    Now, what this is, heaven knows.

MISTRESS LOW-WATER.   Nor can I guess.

    The course of her whole life, and her dead husband's   45
    Was ever full of such dishonest riddles
    To keep right heirs from knowledge of their own.
    And now I'm put i'th' mind on't, I believe
    It was some piece of land or money given
    By some departing friend upon their deathbed,   50
    Perhaps to yourself, and Sir Oliver's daughter
    May wrongfully enjoy it, and she hired
    (For she was but an hireling in those days)
    To keep the injury secret.

JANE.   The most likeliest
    That ever you could think on.

MISTRESS LOW-WATER.   Is it not?   55

JANE.

    Sure, coz. I think you have untied the knot;
    My thoughts lie at more ease. As in all other things,
    In this I thank your help and may you live
    To conquer your own troubles, and cross ends,
    As you are ready to supply your friends.   60

MISTRESS LOW-WATER.

    I thank you for the kind truth of your heart,
    In which I flourish when all means depart.—
    [Aside.] Sure in that oath of hers there sleeps some wrong
    Done to my kinswoman.

               Enter Footman.

JANE.   Who'd you speak withal?

FOOTMAN.

    The gentlewoman of this house, forsooth.   65

---

49. piece] *Dyce;* price *O.*   60. you] *Dyce;* your *O.*

JANE.

Whose footman are you?

FOOTMAN.   One Sir Gilbert Lambston's.

JANE.

Sir Gilbert Lambston's? There my cousin walks.

FOOTMAN.

Thank your good worship.   [*Exit* Jane.]

MISTRESS LOW-WATER.   How now, whence are you?

FOOTMAN.

This letter will make known.   [*Gives letter to her.*]

MISTRESS LOW-WATER.   Whence comes it, sir?

FOOTMAN.

From the knight, my master, Sir Gilbert Lambston.   70

MISTRESS LOW-WATER.

Return't; I'll receive none on't.   [*Throws down letter.*]

FOOTMAN.   There it must lie then;

I were as good run to Tyburn afoot and hang myself

At mine own charges as carry it back again.   *Exit.*

MISTRESS LOW-WATER.

Life, had he not his answer? What strange impudence

Governs in man, when lust is lord of him?   75

Thinks he me mad? 'Cause I have no moneys on earth,

That I'll go forfeit my estate in heaven

And live eternal beggar? He shall pardon me,

That's my soul's jointure; I'll starve ere I sell that.

Oh, is he gone, and left the letter here!   80

Yet I will read it, more to hate the writer.   [*Reads.*]

"Mistress Low-water—If you desire to understand your

own comfort, hear me out, ere you refuse me. I'm in the

way now to double the yearly means that first I offered

you; and to stir you more to me, I'll empty your enemy's   85

bags to maintain you; for the rich widow, the Lady Gold-

enfleece, to whom I have been a longer suitor than you

an adversary, hath given me so much encouragement

lately, insomuch that I am perfectly assured, the next

88. an adversary] *Dyce;* a longer
adversary *O.*

---

72. *Tyburn*] where executions by hanging were held.

meeting strikes the bargain. The happiness that follows 90
this 'twere idle to inform you of; only consent to my
desires, and the widow's notch shall lie open to you. Thus
much to your heart; I know y'are wise. Farewell.—Thy
friend to his power, and another's,—Gilbert Lambston."
In this poor brief, what volumes has he thrust   95
Of treacherous perjury and adulterous lust!
So foul a monster does this wrong appear
That I give pity to mine enemy here.
What a most fearful love reigns in some hearts
That dare oppose all judgment to get means,   100
And wed rich widows only to keep queans.
What a strange path he takes to my affection,
And thinks't the near'st way—'twill never be—
Goes through mine enemy's ground to come to me.
This letter is most welcome; I repent now   105
That my last anger threw thee at my feet;
My bosom shall receive thee.

       Enter Sir Gilbert Lambston.

SIR GILBERT [*aside*].   'Tis good policy too,
   To keep one that so mortally hates the widow;
   She'll have more care to keep it close herself.
   And look what wind her revenge goes withal,   110
   The self-same gale whisks up the sails of love.
   I shall loose much good sport by that.—
   Now, my sweet mistress!
MISTRESS LOW-WATER.   Sir Gilbert! You change suits oft,
   You were here in black but lately.
SIR GILBERT.
   My mind ne'er shifts though.
MISTRESS LOW-WATER [*aside*].   A foul mind the whilst.— 115
   But sure, sir, this is but a dissembling glass
   You sent before you; 'tis not possible
   Your heart should follow your hand.

112. loose] *this edn.;* lose *O.*   113. suits] *Dyce;* Suiters *O.*

---

101. *queans*] whores.
110. *look what*] whatever.
112. *loose*] set free.

SIR GILBERT.   Then may both perish!

MISTRESS LOW-WATER.

     Do not wish that so soon, sir. Can you make
     A three-months' love to a rich widow's bed,   120
     And lay her pillow under a quean's head?
     I know you can't, howe'er you may dissemble't;
     You have a heart brought up better.

SIR GILBERT.   Faith, you wrong me in't;
     You shall not find it so. I do protest to thee,
     I will be lord of all my promises,   125
     And ere't be long, thou shalt but turn a key
     And find 'em in thy coffer; for my love,
     In matching with the widow, is but policy
     To strengthen my estate and make me able
     To set off all thy kisses with rewards;   130
     That the worst weather our delights behold,
     It may hail pearl, and shower the widow's gold.

MISTRESS LOW-WATER.

     You talk of a brave world, sir.

SIR GILBERT.   'Twill seem better
     When golden happiness breaks forth itself
     Out of the east port of the widow's chamber.   135

MISTRESS LOW-WATER.

     And here it sets.

SIR GILBERT.   Here shall the downfall be;
     Her wealth shall rise from her, and set in thee.

MISTRESS LOW-WATER.

     You men have th'art to overcome poor women.
     Pray give my thoughts the freedom of one day,
     And all the rest take you.

SIR GILBERT.   I straight obey.—   140
     [*Aside.*] This bird's my own.

                   Exit Sir Gilbert Lambston.

MISTRESS LOW-WATER.

     There is no happiness but has her season,
     Wherein the brightness of her virtue shines;

119.S.P. MISTRESS LOW-WATER] *Dyce;*   135. east port] *Bullen;* vast part
MRS. LAMBST. *O.*   *O.*
                                     143. Wherein] *Bullen;* Herein *O.*

The husk falls off in time that long shuts up
The fruit in a dark prison; so sweeps by   145
The cloud of miseries from wretches' eyes,
That yet, though fall'n, at length they see to rise;
The secret powers work wondrously and duly.

Enter Master Low-water.

MASTER LOW-WATER.
Why, how now, Kate?
MISTRESS LOW-WATER.   Oh, are you come, sir? Husband,
Wake, wake, and let not patience keep thee poor;   150
Rouse up thy spirit from this falling slumber.
Make thy distress seem but a weeping dream,
And this the opening morning of thy comforts.
Wipe the salt dew off from thy careful eyes,
And drink a draught of gladness next thy heart   155
T'expel the infection of all poisonous sorrows.
MASTER LOW-WATER.
You turn me past my senses.
MISTRESS LOW-WATER   Will you but second
The purpose I intend, I'll be first forward.
I crave no more of thee but a following spirit;
Will you but grant me that?
MASTER LOW-WATER.   Why, what's the business   160
That should transport thee thus?
MISTRESS LOW-WATER.   Hope of much good,
No fear of the least ill; take that to comfort thee.
MASTER LOW-WATER.
Yea?
MISTRESS LOW-WATER.
Sleep not on't; this is no slumbering business;
'Tis like the sweating sickness; I must keep   165
Your eyes still wake, y'are gone if once you sleep.

---

159. *following spirit*] willingness to help.
165. *the sweating sickness*] a feverish disease characterized by profuse sweating, frequently resulting in death within twenty-four hours. It was epidemic in the fifteenth and sixteenth centuries *(OED)*.

MASTER LOW-WATER.

    I will not rest then till thou hast thy wishes.

MISTRESS LOW-WATER.

    Peruse this love paper as you go.

MASTER LOW-WATER.   A letter?   *Exeunt.*

[I.iii]   *Enter* Sir Oliver Twilight, *with* Master Sandfield, Philip, *and* Savorwit.

SIR OLIVER.

    Good Master Sandfield, for the great affection

    You bear toward my girl, I am well pleas'd

    You should enjoy her beauty. Heaven forbid, sir,

    That I should cast away a proper gentleman,

    So far in love with a sour mood or so.   5

    No, no;

    I'll not die guilty of a lover's neck-cracking.

    Marry, as for portion, there I leave you, sir,

    To the mercy of your destiny again;

    I'll have no hand in that.

SANDFIELD.   Faith, something, sir;   10

    Be't but t'express your love.

SIR OLIVER.   I have no desire, sir,

    To express my love that way, and so rest satisfied.

    I pray take heed in urging that too much

    You draw not my love from me.

SANDFIELD.   Fates foresee, sir.

SIR OLIVER.

    Faith, then you may go; seek out a high steeple,   15

    Or a deep water; there's no saving of you.

SAVORWIT [*aside*].

    How naturally he plays upon himself!

SIR OLIVER.

    Marry, if a wedding dinner, as I told you,

    And three years' board, well lodg'd in mine house,

    And eating, drinking, and a sleeping portion   20

I.iii.] *Dyce; no scene division in*
O.

[I.iii]

    20. *a sleeping portion*] quarters or, perhaps, a living allowance.

May give you satisfaction, I am your man, sir;
Seek out no other.

SANDFIELD.   I am content to embrace it, sir,
Rather than hazard languishment or ruin.

SIR OLIVER.
I love thee for thy wisdom; such a son-in-law
Will cheer a father's heart. Welcome, sweet Master
    Sandfield.   25
Whither away, boys? Philip?

PHILIP.   To visit my love, sir,
Old Master Sunset's daughter.

SIR OLIVER.   That's my Philip.
Ply't hard, my good boys both, put 'em to't finely.
One day, one dinner, and one house shall join you.

PHILIP. SANDFIELD.
That's our desire, sir.   *Exeunt.*

SIR OLIVER.   Pish! Come hither, Savorwit.   30
Observe my son and bring me word, sweet boy,
Whether h'as a speeding wit or no in wooing.

SAVORWIT.
That will I, sir. —[*Aside.*] That your own eyes might
    tell you.
I think it speedy, your girl has a round belly. *Exit* Savorwit.

SIR OLIVER.
How soon the comfortable shine of joy   35
Breaks through a cloud of grief!
The tears that I let fall for my dead wife
Are dried up with the beams of my girl's fortunes.
Her life, her death, and her ten years' distress,
Are ev'n forgot with me; the love and care   40
That I ought her, her daughter sh'owes it all;
It can but be bestow'd, and there 'tis well.

Enter Servant.

26.] *a redundant S.D.* Enter Philip   41. sh'owes] *Bullen;* shows *O.*
printed in O.

---

32. *speeding*] effective.
41. *ought*] owed.
41. *sh'owes*] she owns.

SIR OLIVER.
    How now, what news?
SERVANT.
    There's a Dutch merchant, sir, that's now come over,
    Desires some conference with you.
SIR OLIVER.   How? A Dutch merchant?   45
    Pray send him in to me. —What news with him, trow?
                                          [*Exit* Servant.]

Enter Dutch Merchant *with a little* Dutch Boy *in great slops.*

DUTCH MERCHANT.
    Sir Oliver Twilight?
SIR OLIVER.   That's my name indeed, sir.
    I pray be covered, sir; y'are very welcome.
DUTCH MERCHANT.
    This is my business, sir. I took into my charge
    A few words to deliver to yourself   50
    From a dear friend of yours that wonders strangely
    At your unkind neglect.
SIR OLIVER.   Indeed? What might he be, sir?
DUTCH MERCHANT.
    Nay, y'are i'th' wrong gender now;
    'Tis that distressed lady, your good wife, sir.
SIR OLIVER.
    What say you, sir? My wife?
DUTCH MERCHANT.   Yes, sir, your wife!   55
    This strangeness now of yours seems more to harden
    Th'uncharitable neglect she tax'd you for.
SIR OLIVER.
    Pray give me leave, sir. Is my wife alive?
DUTCH MERCHANT.
    Came any news to you, sir, to th' contrary?
SIR OLIVER.
    Yes, by my faith, did there.
DUTCH MERCHANT.   Pray, how long since, sir?   60
SIR OLIVER.
    'Tis now some ten weeks.

---

46. *trow*] think you.
46.2. *great slops*] wide baggy trousers.

DUTCH MERCHANT.   Faith, within this month, sir,
   I saw her talk and eat; and those in our calendar
   Are signs of life and health.
SIR OLIVER.   Mass, so they are in ours.
DUTCH MERCHANT.
   And these were the last words her passion threw me:
   No grief, quoth she, sits to my heart so close   65
   As his unkindness and my daughter's loss.
SIR OLIVER.
   You make me weep and wonder, for I swear
   I sent her ransom, and that daughter's here.
DUTCH MERCHANT.
   Here! That will come well to lighten her of one grief.
   I long to see her for the piteous moan   70
   Her mother made for her.
SIR OLIVER.   That shall you, sir. —Within there!

[*Enter* Servant.]

SERVANT.
   Sir?
SIR OLIVER. Call down my daughter.
SERVANT.   Yes, sir.   [*Exit.*]
SIR OLIVER.
   Here's strange budgelling! I tell you, sir,
   Those that I put in trust were near me, too—
   A man would think they should not juggle with me—   75
   My own son, and my servant, no worse people, sir.
DUTCH MERCHANT.
   And yet, ofttimes, sir, what worse knave to a man
   Than he that eats his meat?
SIR OLIVER.   Troth, you say true, sir.
   I sent 'em simply, and that news they brought,
   My wife had left the world; and with that sum   80
   I sent to her, this brought his sister home.
   Look you, sir, this is she.

80. sum] *Bullen;* Son *O.*

---

  64. *passion*] sorrow.
  73. *budgelling*] equivocating.
  80. *sum*] the ransom money.

Enter Grace.

DUTCH MERCHANT.   If my eye sin not, sir,
    Or misty error falsify the glass,
    I saw that face at Antwerp in an inn
    When I set forth first to fetch home this boy.   85
SIR OLIVER.
    How? In an inn?
GRACE [*aside*].   Oh, I am betray'd, I fear.
DUTCH MERCHANT.
    How do you, young mistress?
GRACE.   Your eyes wrong your tongue, sir,
    And makes you sin in both; I am not she.
DUTCH MERCHANT.
    No? Then I never saw face twice. —Sir Oliver Twilight,
    I tell you my free thoughts, I fear y'are blinded.   90
    I do not like this story; I doubt much
    The sister is as false as the dead mother.
SIR OLIVER.
    Yea! Say you so, sir? I see nothing lets me,
    But to doubt so too then.—
    So, to your chamber; we have done with you.   95
GRACE [*aside*].
    I would be glad you had. Here's a strange storm.—
    Sift it out well, sir; till anon I leave you, sir.   [*Exit.*]
DUTCH MERCHANT.
    Business commands me hence, but as a pledge
    Of my return, I'll leave my little son with you,
    Who yet takes little pleasure in this country   100
    'Cause he can speak no English, all Dutch he.
SIR OLIVER.
    A fine boy; he's welcome, sir, to me.
DUTCH MERCHANT.
    Where's your leg and your thanks to the gentleman?
    War es you neighgen an you thonkes you?

104.] *this edn.; spoken by Dutch
Boy in O.*

---

93. *lets*] hinders.
104–5. *War . . . kite.*] The Dutch spoken by the merchant and his
boy is a stage representation of the language and is intended to be

DUTCH BOY.

    Ick donck you, ver ew edermon vrendly kite.   105

SIR OLIVER.

    What says he, sir?

DUTCH MERCHANT.   He thanks you for your kindness.

SIR OLIVER.   Pretty knave!

DUTCH MERCHANT.

    Had not some business held me by the way,

    This news had come to your ear ten days ago.

SIR OLIVER.

    It comes too soon now, methinks; I'm your debtor.

DUTCH MERCHANT.

    But I could wish it, sir, for better ware.   *Exit.* 110

SIR OLIVER.

    We must not be our own choosers in our fortunes.

    Here's a cold pie to breakfast: wife alive,

    The daughter doubtful, and the money spent!

    How am I juggled withal?

               Enter Savorwit.

SAVORWIT.   It hits i'faith, sir;

    The work goes even.

SIR OLIVER.   Oh, come, come, come, are you come, sir? 115

SAVORWIT [*aside*].

    Life, what's the matter now?

SIR OLIVER.

    There's a new reckoning come in since.

SAVORWIT [*aside*].

    Pox on't! I thought all had been paid;

    I can't abide these after-reckonings.

SIR OLIVER.

    I pray come near sir; let's be acquainted with you.   120

    You're bold enough abroad with my purse, sir.

SAVORWIT.

    No more than beseems manners and good use, sir.

---

somewhat comprehensible. The Dutch that Savorwit "gabbles," ll. 143
ff., is strictly for laughs. Line 104 is a translation into "Dutch" of l.
103.

    110. *ware*] merchandise.

SIR OLIVER.
  Did not you bring me word some ten weeks since,
  My wife was dead?
SAVORWIT.   Yes, true, sir, very true, sir.
SIR OLIVER.
  Pray stay, and take my horse along with you!   125
  And with the ransom that I sent for her
  That you redeem'd my daughter?
SAVORWIT.   Right as can be, sir;
  I never found your worship in a false tale yet.
SIR OLIVER.
  I thank you for your good word, sir, but I'm like
  To find your worship now in two at once.   130
SAVORWIT.
  I should be sorry to hear that.
SIR OLIVER.   I believe you, sir.
  Within this month my wife was sure alive—
  There's six weeks bated of your ten-weeks' lie—
  As has been credibly reported to me
  By a Dutch merchant, father to that boy,   135
  But now come over, and the words scarce cold.
SAVORWIT [aside].
  Oh, strange! —'Tis a most rank untruth; where is he, sir?
SIR OLIVER.
  He will not be long absent.
SAVORWIT [aside].   All's confounded.—
  If he were here, I'll tell him to his face, sir;
  He wears a double tongue—that's Dutch and English.   140
  Will the boy say't?
SIR OLIVER.   'Las, he can speak no English.
SAVORWIT [aside].
  All the better; I'll gabble something to him.—
  Hoyste kaloiste, kalooskin ee vou, dar sune, alla gaskin?
DUTCH BOY.
  Ick wet neat watt hey zackt; Ick unverston ewe neat.
SAVORWIT.
  Why la, I thought as much.
SIR OLIVER.   What says the boy?   145

SAVORWIT.

He says his father is troubled with an imperfection at
one time of the moon and talks like a madman.

SIR OLIVER.

What? Does the boy say so?

SAVORWIT.   I knew there was somewhat in't.
Your wife alive! Will you believe all tales, sir?

SIR OLIVER.

Nay, more, sir; he told me he saw this wench,   150
Which you brought home, at Antwerp in an inn;
Tells me, I'm plainly cozen'd of all hands;
'Tis not my daughter neither.

SAVORWIT [aside].   All's broke out.—
How? Not your daughter, sir? I must to't again.
Quisquinikin sadlamare, alla pisse kickin sows-clows, hoff 155
tofte le cumber shaw, bouns bus boxsceeno.

DUTCH BOY.

Ick an sawth no int hein clappon de heeke, I dinke ute
zein zennon.

SAVORWIT.

Oh, *zein zennon!* Ah ha! I thought how 'twould prove
i'th' end. The boy says they never came near Antwerp, a 160
quite contrary way, round about by Parma.

SIR OLIVER.

What's the same *zein zennon?*

SAVORWIT.

That is, he saw no such wench in an inn. 'Tis well I
came in such happy time to get it out of the boy before
his father returned again; pray be wary, sir; the world's 165
subtle; come and pretend a charitable business in policy,
and work out a piece of money on you.

SIR OLIVER.

Mass, art advis'd of that?

SAVORWIT.

The age is cunning, sir, beside a Dutchman will live
upon any ground, and work butter out of a thistle.   170

152. Tells] *Dyce;* Tell *O.*

---

151. *Antwerp]* center of the English wool trade in Flanders.
161. *Parma]* city in Italy, certainly "round about."
170. *butter . . . thistle]* stereotyped English concept of fat Dutchmen.

SIR OLIVER.

Troth, thou say'st true in that; they're the best thrivers
in turnips, hartichalks, and cabishes; our English are
not like them.

SAVORWIT.

Oh, fie, no, sir!

SIR OLIVER.

Ask him from whence they came, when they came hither. 175

SAVORWIT.

That I will sir. —*Culluaron lagooso, lageen, lagan, rufft,
punkatee.*

DUTCH BOY.

Nimd aweigh de cack.

SAVORWIT.

What, what? I cannot blame him then.

SIR OLIVER.

What says he to thee? 180

SAVORWIT.

The poor boy blushes for him; he tells me his father came
from making merry with certain of his countrymen and
he's a little steep'd in English beer. There's no heed to
be taken of his tongue now.

SIR OLIVER.

Hoyda! How com'st thou by all this? I heard him speak 185
but three words to thee?

SAVORWIT.

Oh, sir, the Dutch is a very wide language. You shall
have ten English words even for one, as for example,
Gullder-goose; there's a word for you, master.

SIR OLIVER.

Why, what's that same *Gullder-goose*? 190

SAVORWIT.

How do you and all your generation.

SIR OLIVER.

Why, 'tis impossible! How prove you that, sir?

---

172. *hartichalks*] artichokes.
172. *cabishes*] cabbages.

SAVORWIT.

    'Tis thus distinguish'd, sir: *Gull,* how do you—*der,* and—
    goose, your generation.

SIR OLIVER.

    'Tis a most saucy language; how cam'st thou by't?   195

SAVORWIT.

    I was brought up to London in an eelship;
    There was the place I caught it first by th' tail.—
    [*Aside.*] I shall be tripp'd anon; pox, would I were gone.—
    I'll go seek out your son, sir, you shall hear
    What thunder he'll bring with him.

SIR OLIVER.   Do, do, Savorwit;   200
    I'll have you all face to face.

SAVORWIT [*aside*].   Cuds me! What else, sir?
    And you take me so near the net again,
    I'll give you leave to squat me; I have 'scap'd fairly.
    We are undone in Dutch; all our three-months' roguery
    Is now come over in a butter firkin.   *Exit* Savorwit. 205

SIR OLIVER.

    Never was man so toss'd between two tales!
    I know not which to take, not which to trust;
    The boy here is the likeliest to tell truth,
    Because the world's corruption is not yet
    At full years in him; sure he cannot know   210
    What deceit means, 'tis English yet to him.
    And when I think again, why should the father
    Dissemble for no profit? He gets none,
    Whate'er he hopes for, and I think he hopes not.
    The man's in a good case, being old and weary,   215
    He dares not lean his arm on his son's shoulder,
    For fear he lie i'th' dirt, but must be rather
    Beholding to a stranger for his prop.

197. tail] *Dyce;* tale *O.*

---

196. *eelship*] The Dutch were credited with a taste for eels.
201. *Cuds me*] i.e., God's me, one of Middleton's favorite expletives.
203. *squat*] "Jamieson *(Sup. to Et. Dict. of Scot. Lang.)* gives 'Squat,
to strike with the open hand, particularly on the breech,' in which
sense the word seems to be used above" (Dyce).
205. *firkin*] small cask.
215. *in a good case*] well off, used ironically.

Enter Dutchman [Dutch Merchant].

DUTCH MERCHANT.
> I make bold once again, sir, for a boy here.

SIR OLIVER.
> Oh, sir, y'are welcome. Pray resolve me one thing, sir;   220
> Did you within this month, with your own eyes,
> See my wife living?

DUTCH MERCHANT.   I ne'er borrowed any.
> Why should you move that question, sir? Dissembling
> Is no part of my living.

SIR OLIVER.   I have reason
> To urge it so far, sir—pray be not angry though—   225
> Because my man was here since your departure,
> Withstands all stiffly, and to make it clearer,
> Question'd your boy in Dutch, who, as he told me,
> Return'd this answer first to him: that you
> Had imperfection at one time o'th' moon   230
> Which made you talk so strangely.

DUTCH MERCHANT.
> How, how's this? *Zeicke yongon, ick ben ick quelt medien*
> *dullek heght, ee untoit van the mon, an koot uram'd?*

DUTCH BOY.
> *Wee ek, heigh lieght in ze bokkas, dee't site.*

DUTCH MERCHANT.
> Why, la you, sir! Here's no such thing;   235
> He says he lies in's throat that says it.

SIR OLIVER.
> Then the rogue lies in's throat, for he told me so,
> And that the boy should answer at next question
> That you ne'er saw this wench, nor came near Antwerp.

DUTCH MERCHANT.
> Ten thousand devils! *Zeicke hee ewe ek kneeght, yongon,*   240
> *dat wee neeky by Antwarpon ne don cammen no seene*
> *de doughter dor?*

DUTCH BOY.
> *Ick hub ham hean sulka dongon he zaut, hei es an*
> *skallom an rubbout.*

---

220. *resolve*] satisfy.

DUTCH MERCHANT.

He says he told him no such matter; he's a knave and a 245
rascal.

SIR OLIVER.

Why, how am I abus'd? Pray tell me one thing,
What's *Gullder-goose* in Dutch?

DUTCH MERCHANT.

How? *Gullder-goose?* There's no such thing in Dutch; it
may be an ass in English.   250

SIR OLIVER.

Hoyda! Then am I that ass in plain English; I am grossly
cozen'd, most inconsiderately!
Pray let my house receive you for one night
That I may quit these rascals, I beseech you, sir.

DUTCH MERCHANT.

If that may stead you, sir; I'll not refuse you.   255

SIR OLIVER.

A thousand thanks, and welcome.
On whom can fortune more spit out her foam,
Work'd on abroad, and play'd upon at home   *Exeunt.*

[II.i]
Enter Weatherwise, *the gull, meeting* [Pickadille *and*] *two or
three* [servants] *bringing out a table.*

WEATHERWISE.

So, set the table ready; the widow's i'th' next room, look-
ing upon my clock with the days and the months and the
change of the moon. I'll fetch her in presently.   [*Exit.*]

PICKADILLE.

She's not so mad to be fetch'd in with the moon, I warrant you. A man must go roundlier to work with a widow   5
than to woo her with the hand of a dial, or stir up her
blood with the striking part of a clock; I should ne'er
stand to show her such things in chamber.
                                        Exeunt [Servants].

Enter Weatherwise *with the widow* [Lady Goldenfleece], Sir Gilbert Lambston, Master Pepperton, [*and*] Master Overdon.

---

254. *quit*] requite.

WEATHERWISE.

Welcome, sweet widow, to a bachelor's house here; a
single man I, but for two or three maids that I keep.   10

LADY GOLDENFLEECE.

Why, are you double with them then?

WEATHERWISE.

An exceeding good mourning wit! Women are wiser than
ever they were, since they wore doublets. You must think,
sweet widow, if a man keep maids, they're under his
subjection.   15

LADY GOLDENFLEECE.

That's most true, sir.

WEATHERWISE.

They have no reason to have a lock but the master must
have a key to't.

LADY GOLDENFLEECE.

To him, Sir Gilbert. He fights with me at a wrong
weapon now.   20

WEATHERWISE [aside].

Nay, and Sir Gilbert strike, my weapon falls;
I fear no thrust but his. Here are more shooters,
But they have shot two arrows without heads;
They cannot stick i'th' butt yet. Hold out, knight,
And I'll cleave the black pin i'th' midst o'th' white.   25
                                                      Exit.

LADY GOLDENFLEECE.

Nay, and he led me into a closet, sir, where he showed

---

11. *double*] deceitful.

13. *since . . . doublets*] a new outrageous fashion of women wearing
men's clothes.

17–18. *lock . . . key*] Epigram 404 of Sir John Harington bawdily
refers to a knight having the "kaye" to his lady's "cabbinett."

21. *and*] if; frequently used, hereafter not glossed.

22. *shooters*] pun on suitors which was pronounced the same.

24. *butt*] one of the three kinds of targets used in archery: "Buts,
Pricks, or Rovers" (Cotton).

25. *cleave . . . white*] "The *white* was the inner circle of the target,
and the *pin* [peg] stood in the centre of the *white*. Hence to *cleave
the pin* was the highest feat in archery" (Bullen).

me diet drinks for several months, as scurvigrass for
April, clarified whey for June, and the like.

SIR GILBERT.

Oh, madam, he is a most necessary property, an't be but
to save our credit, ten pound in a banquet.   30

LADY GOLDENFLEECE.

Go, y'are a wag, Sir Gilbert.

SIR GILBERT.

How many there be in the world of his fortunes that
prick their own calves with briers to make an easy passage for others, or like a toiling usurer sets his son a-
horse-back in cloth-of-gold breeches while he himself goes   35
t'th' devil a-foot in a pair of old strossers.
But shall I give a more familiar sign?
His are the sweetmeats, but the kisses mine.   [*Kisses her.*]

MASTER OVERDON.

Excellent—[*aside*] a pox o' your fortune.

MASTER PEPPERTON [*to* Master Overdon].

Saucy courting has brought all modest wooing clean out   40
of fashion. You shall have few maids nowadays got without rough handling; all the town's so us'd to't, and most
commonly too they're join'd before they're married,
because they'll be sure to be fast enough.

MASTER OVERDON.

Sir, since he strives t'oppose himself against us,   45
Let's so combine our friendships in our straits,
By all means graceful to assist each other.
For I protest it shall as much glad me
To see your happiness and his disgrace,
As if the wealth were mine, the love, the place.   50

MASTER PEPPERTON.

And with the like faith I reward your friendship.
I'll break the bawdy ranks of his discourse

---

27. *scurvigrass*] a plant which was believed to possess antiscurvy
properties.
28. *clarified whey*] along with "physics," l. 70, traditional home
remedies for health.
29. *an't*] if it, frequently used, hereafter not glossed.
36. *strossers*] tight breeches.

And scatter his libidinous whispers straight.—
Madam!

LADY GOLDENFLEECE.   How cheer you, gentlemen?

SIR GILBERT [aside].   Pox on 'em,
They wak'd me out of a fine sleep; three minutes   55
Had fasten'd all the treasure in mine arms.

MASTER PEPPERTON.

You took no note of this conceit, it seems, madam.

LADY GOLDENFLEECE.

Twelve trenchers, upon every one a month.
January, February, March, April—

MASTER PEPPERTON.

Ay, and their poesies under 'em.   60

LADY GOLDENFLEECE.

Pray, what says May? She's the spring lady.

MASTER PEPPERTON.

"Now gallant May in her array,
Doth make the field pleasant and gay."

MASTER OVERDON.

"This month of June use clarified whey,
Boil'd with cold herbs, and drink alway."   65

LADY GOLDENFLEECE.

Drink't all away, he should say.

MASTER PEPPERTON.

'Twere much better indeed, and wholesomer for his liver.

SIR GILBERT.

September's a good one here, madam.

LADY GOLDENFLEECE.

Oh, have you chose your month; let's hear't, Sir Gilbert.

SIR GILBERT.

"Now mayst thou physics safely take,   70
And bleed, and bathe for thy health's sake.

62.S.P. MASTER PEPPERTON] Dyce;
not in O.

---

60. poesies] "like Epigrammes that were . . . put vpon their banket-
ting dishes, . . . we call them Posies, and do paint them nowadays
vpon the backe sides of our fruit trenchers of wood" (Puttenham, p. 47).

Eat figs and grapes and spicery,
For to refresh thy members dry."

LADY GOLDENFLEECE.

Thus it is still, when a man's simple meaning lights
among wantons. How many honest words have suffered   75
corruption since Chaucer's days? A virgin would speak
those words then that a very midwife would blush to
hear now, if she have but so much blood left to make up
an ounce of grace. And who is this long on, but such
wags as you that use your words like your wenches. You   80
cannot let 'em pass honestly by you, but you must still
have a flirt at 'em.

MASTER PEPPERTON.

You have paid some of us home, madam.

Enter Weatherwise.

WEATHERWISE [*aside*].

If conceit will strike this stroke, have at the widow's
plumtree. I'll put 'em down all for a banquet. —Widow   85
and gentlemen, my friends and servants, I make you
wait long here for a bachelor's pittance.

LADY GOLDENFLEECE.

Oh, sir, y'are pleas'd to be modest.

WEATHERWISE.

No, by my troth, widow. You shall find it otherwise.

*Strike music. Enter banquet, and six of his tenants with the
twelve signs, made like banqueting-stuff. Aries, Taurus, Gemini,
Cancer, Leo, Virgo, Libra, Scorpio, Sagittarius, Capricorn, Aquarius, and Pisces.*

LADY GOLDENFLEECE.

What, the twelve signs?   90

---

73. *members*] the double entendre which causes the widow's com-
plaint, ll. 74–82; cf. Doll's comments on the word "occupy" in *II Henry
IV*, II.iv.159–62.

79. *long on*] because of.

85. *plumtree*] "one of the many cant terms for the *pudendum
muliebre*" (Bullen).

89.1. *banquet*] not a feast, but an elaborate dessert *(OED)*.

WEATHERWISE.

These are the signs of my love, widow.

LADY GOLDENFLEECE.

Worse meat would have serv'd us, sir. By my faith,
I'm sorry you should be at such charges, sir,
To feast us a whole month together here.

WEATHERWISE.

Widow, thou'rt welcome a whole month, and ever.   95

LADY GOLDENFLEECE.

And what be those, sir, that brought in the banquet?

WEATHERWISE.

Those are my tenants; they stand for fasting days.

SIR GILBERT.

Or the six weeks in Lent.

WEATHERWISE.   Y'are i'th' right, Sir Gilbert.
Sweet widow, take your place at Aries here;
That's the head sign. A widow is the head   100
Till she be married.

LADY GOLDENFLEECE.   What is she then?

WEATHERWISE.   The middle.

LADY GOLDENFLEECE.

'Tis happy she's no worse.   [Sits.]

WEATHERWISE.

Taurus, Sir Gilbert Lambston, that's for you.
They say you're a good town-bull.

SIR GILBERT.   Oh, spare your friends, sir.   [Sits.]

WEATHERWISE.

And Gemini for Master Pepperton.   105
He had two boys at once by his last wife.

MASTER PEPPERTON.

I hear the widow find no fault with that, sir.   [Sits.]

WEATHERWISE.

Cancer the Crab for Master Overdon,
For when a thing's past fifty, it grows crooked. [Overton sits.]

LADY GOLDENFLEECE.

Now for yourself, sir.

99–100. *Aries . . . head sign*] Most of Weatherwise's comments are
puns on the characteristics of the zodiacal signs.
104. *town-bull*] a whore master.

WEATHERWISE.   Take no care for me, widow;   110
  I can be anywhere. Here's Leo,
  Heart and back; Virgo, guts and belly.
  I can go lower yet, and yet fare better,
  Since Sagittarius fits me the thighs;
  I care not if I be about the thighs,   115
  I shall find meat enough.   [*Sits.*]
LADY GOLDENFLEECE.   But under pardon, sir.
  Though you be Lord o'th' feast, and the conceit both,
  Methinks it had been proper for the banquet
  To have had the signs all fill'd, and no one idle.
WEATHERWISE.
  I know it had, but whose fault's that, widow? You should 120
  have got you more suitors to have stopp'd the gaps.
LADY GOLDENFLEECE.
  Nay sure, they should get us, and not we them.
  There be your tenants, sir; we are not proud;
  You may bid them sit down.
WEATHERWISE.
  By th' mass, it's true too. Then sit down tenants once 125
  with your hats on, but spare the meat, I charge you as
  you hope for new leases. I must make my signs draw out
  a month yet, with a bit every morning to breakfast, and
  at full moon with a whole one; that's restorative. Sit
  round, sit round, and do not speak, sweet tenants. You 130
  may be bold enough, so you eat but little.   [*Tenants sit.*]
  How like you this now, widow?
LADY GOLDENFLEECE.   It shows well, sir;
  And like the good old hospitable fashion.
PICKADILLE [*aside*].
  How! Like a good old hospital! My mistress makes an
  arrant gull on him.   135
LADY GOLDENFLEECE.
  But yet methinks there wants clothes for the feet.

111–16. I can be . . . enough] *this
edn.; in O lines end* Vir-/ fare/
thighs;/ I/ meat/ enough.

---

136. *clothes for the feet*] a cover [guest] for Pisces.

WEATHERWISE.

That part's uncovered yet. Push! no matter for the feet.

LADY GOLDENFLEECE.

Yes, if the feet catch cold, the head will feel it.

WEATHERWISE.

Why then, you may draw up your legs, and lie rounder
together.   140

SIR GILBERT.

H'as answered you well, madam.

WEATHERWISE.

And you draw up your legs too, widow, my tenant will
feel you there, for he's one of the calves.

LADY GOLDENFLEECE.

Better and better, sir; your wit fattens as he feeds.

PICKADILLE [aside].

Sh'as took the calf from his tenant and put it upon his 145
ground now.

[Enter Servant.]

WEATHERWISE.

How now, my lady's man, what's the news, sir?

SERVANT.

Madam, there's a young gentleman below;
H'as earnest business to your ladyship.

WEATHERWISE.

Another suitor, I hold my life, widow.   150

LADY GOLDENFLEECE.

What is he, sir?

SERVANT.   He seems a gentleman,
That's the least of him, and yet more I know not.

LADY GOLDENFLEECE.

Under the leave o'th' master of the house here,
I would he were admitted.

WEATHERWISE.

With all my heart, widow; I fear him not.   155
Come cut and long tail!   [Exit Servant.]

SIR GILBERT [aside].   I have the least fear,
And the most firmness; nothing can shake me.

---

156. *Come cut and long tail*] a common proverb meaning come all
kinds.

WEATHERWISE.

If he be a gentleman, he's welcome; there's a sign does
nothing, and that's fit for a gentleman. The feet will be
kept warm enough now for you, widow, for if he be a   160
right gentleman, he has his stockings warm'd and he
wears socks beside, partly for warmth, partly for cleanli-
ness; and if he observe Fridays too, he comes excellent
well. Pisces will be a fine fish dinner for him.

LADY GOLDENFLEECE.

Why then you mean, sir, he shall sit as he comes?   165

WEATHERWISE.

Ay, and he were a lord, he shall not sit above my tenants.
I'll not have two lords to them, so I may go look my rent
in another man's breeches. I was not brought up to be so
unmannerly.

Enter Mistress Low-water *as a gallant gentleman, her husband*
[Master Low-water] *like a serving-man after her.*

MISTRESS LOW-WATER [*aside*].

　I have pick'd out a bold time.—   170
　Much good do you, gentlemen.

WEATHERWISE.   Y'are welcome as I may say, sir.

MISTRESS LOW-WATER.

Pardon my rudeness, madam.

LADY GOLDENFLEECE.   No such fault, sir;

You're too severe to yourself; our judgment quits you.
Please you to do as we do.

MISTRESS LOW-WATER.   Thanks, good madam.

LADY GOLDENFLEECE.

Make room, gentlemen.

WEATHERWISE.   Sit still, tenants.   175

I'll call in all your old leases, and rack you else.

169.1–2.] *after l. 146 in* O; *a re-*　　　*edn.; in* O *lines end* much/ Gen-
dundant S.D. Enter Mistress Low-　　　tlemen.
water *printed here in* O.　　　　　　175–76.] *this edn.; in* O *lines end*
170–71. I . . . gentlemen] *this*　　　Gentlemen./ old/ else.

---

162. *wears socks beside*] the mark of a gentleman (Brooke, p. 64).
176. *rack*] extort.

ALL TENANTS.

    Oh, sweet landlord!

MISTRESS LOW-WATER.

    Take my cloak, sirrah.—   *Gives cloak to* Master Low-water.
                      If any be disturb'd,
    I'll not sit, gentlemen. I see my place.

WEATHERWISE [*aside*].

    A proper woman turn'd gallant! If the widow refuse me, 180
    I care not if I be a suitor to him. I have known those
    who have been as mad, and given half their living for a
    male companion.

MISTRESS LOW-WATER.

    How, Pisces! Is that mine? 'Tis a conceited banquet.   [*Sits.*]

WEATHERWISE.

    If you love any fish, pray fall to, sir. If you had come 185
    sooner, you might have happened among some of the
    flesh signs, but now they're all taken up; Virgo had been
    a good dish for you, had not one of my tenants been
    somewhat busy with her.

MISTRESS LOW-WATER.

    Pray let him keep her, sir; give me meat fresh,   190
    I'd rather have whole fish than broken flesh.

SIR GILBERT.

    What say you to a bit of Taurus?

MISTRESS LOW-WATER.   No, I thank you, sir;
    The bull's too rank for me.

SIR GILBERT.   How, sir?

MISTRESS LOW-WATER.   Too rank, sir.

SIR GILBERT.

    Fie, I shall strike you dumb like all your fellows.

MISTRESS LOW-WATER.

    What, with your heels or horns?

SIR GILBERT.   Perhaps with both.   195

MISTRESS LOW-WATER.

    It must be at dead low water, when I'm dead then.

178–79.] *Dyce; in* O *lines end* di- /
Gentlemen,/ place.
184.] *Dyce; 2 lines in* O, *ending*
mine?/ Banquet.

196. low water] *Dyce;* Low-water
O.

MASTER LOW-WATER [*aside*].

> 'Tis brave, Kate, and nobly spoke of thee.

WEATHERWISE.

> This quarrel must be drown'd. —Pickadille, my lady's
> fool!

PICKADILLE.

> You're your own man, sir.   200

WEATHERWISE.

> Prithee, step in to one o'th' maids.

PICKADILLE.

> That I will, sir, and thank you, too.

WEATHERWISE.

> Nay, hark you, sir; call for my sun-cup presently; I'd
> forgot it.

PICKADILLE.

> How, your sun-cup? —[*Aside*.] Some cup I warrant that 205
> he stole out o'th' Sun Tavern.   [*Exit.*]

LADY GOLDENFLEECE [*aside*].

> The more I look on him, the more I thirst for't.
> Methinks his beauty does so far transcend,
> Turns the signs back, makes that the upper end.

WEATHERWISE.

> How cheer you, widow? Gentlemen, how cheer you?   210
> Fair weather in all quarters!
> The sun will peep anon; I have sent one for him.
> In the meantime I'll tell you a tale of these.
> This Libra here that keeps the scale so even
> Was i'th' old time an honest chandler's widow   215
> And had one daughter which was called Virgo,
> Which now my hungry tenant has deflower'd.
> This Virgo, passing for a maid, was sued to
> By Sagittarius there, a gallant shooter,
> And Aries, his head rival; but her old crabbed   220
> Uncle Cancer here, dwelling in Crooked Lane,

---

206. *Sun Tavern*] located in New Fish Street; see pun at l. 287.
207. *him*] the disguised Mistress Low-water.
221. *Crooked Lane*] a street which formerly ran from New Fish Street to St. Michael's Lane (Sugden).

Still cross'd the marriage, minding to bestow her
Upon one Scorpio, a rich usurer.
The girl, loathing that match, fell into folly
With one Taurus, a gentleman in Townbull Street,   225
By whom she had two twins, those Gemini there,
Of which two brats, she was brought a-bed in Leo,
At the Red Lion about Tower Hill.
Being in this distress, one Capricorn,
An honest citizen, pitied her case and married her   230
To Aquarius, an old water-bearer,
And Pisces was her living ever after;
At Standard she sold fish where he drew water.

ALL.

It shall be yours, sir.

LADY GOLDENFLEECE.   Meat and mirth too! Y'are lavish.
Your purse and tongue has been at cost today, sir.   235

SIR GILBERT.

You may challenge all comers at these twelve weapons, I
warrant you.

Enter Clown [Pickadille, *carrying the sun-cup, wearing no doublet, but wearing a veil over his face*].

PICKADILLE.

Your sun-cup call you it! 'Tis a simple voyage that I have
made here. I have left my doublet within for fear I
should sweat through my jerkin, and thrown a cypress 240
over my face for fear of sun burning.

WEATHERWISE.

How now, who's this? Why, sirrah!

PICKADILLE.

Can you endure it, mistress?

LADY GOLDENFLEECE.

Endure what, fool?

242. who's] *Dyce;* whose *O.*

---

225. *Townbull Street*] a jocular substitute for Turnbull Street, an
infamous quarter of the town (Bullen).
228. *Red Lion*] a pub near the Tower of London (Sugden).
233. *Standard*] "a water conduit in Cheapside" (Sugden).
240. *cypress*] a dark veil.

WEATHERWISE.

    Fill the cup, coxcomb.   245

PICKADILLE.

    Nay, an't be no hotter, I'll go put on my doublet again. *Exit.*

WEATHERWISE.

    What a whoreson sot is this! Prithee, fill the cup, fellow,
    and give't the widow.   [*Gives cup to* Master Low-water.]

MISTRESS LOW-WATER.

    Sirrah, how stand you? Bestow your service there upon
    her ladyship.   [*He gives* Lady Goldenfleece *the cup.*] 250

LADY GOLDENFLEECE.

    What's here? a sun?

WEATHERWISE.   It does betoken, madam,
    A cheerful day to somebody.

LADY GOLDENFLEECE [*aside*].   It rises
    Full in the face of yon fair sign, and yet
    By course he is the last must feel the heat.—
    Here, gentlemen, to you all,   255
    For you know the sun must go through the twelve signs.
                               [*Drinks.*]

WEATHERWISE.

    Most wittily, widow; you jump with my conceit right;
    There's not a hair between us.

LADY GOLDENFLEECE.   Give it Sir Gilbert.

SIR GILBERT.

    I am the next through whom the golden flame
    Shines, when 'tis spent in thy celestial ram.   260
    The poor feet there must wait and cool a while.   [*Drinks.*]

MISTRESS LOW-WATER.

    We have our time, sir; joy and we shall meet;
    I have known the proud neck lie between the feet.

WEATHERWISE.

    So round it goes.   [*Each drinks in turn.*]

      Enter Clown [Pickadille].

253. yon] *Dyce;* you *O.*

263. *proud neck . . . feet*] Taurus (Sir Gilbert) dominates the neck;
Pisces (Mrs. Low-water), the feet.

PICKADILLE.   I like this drinking world well.

WEATHERWISE.

    So fill't him again.

MASTER PEPPERTON.   Fill't me? Why, I drunk last, sir.   265

WEATHERWISE.

    I know you did, but Gemini must drink twice,

    Unless you mean that one of them shall be chok'd.

LADY GOLDENFLEECE [aside].

    Fly from my heart all variable thoughts.

    She that's entic'd by every pleasing object

    Shall find small pleasure, and as little rest.   270

    This knave hath lov'd me long; he's best and worthiest,

    I cannot but in honor see him requited.—

    Sir Gilbert Lambston!

MISTRESS LOW-WATER.   How! Pardon me, sweet lady,

    That with a bold tongue I strike by your words,

    Sir Gilbert Lambston?

SIR GILBERT.   Yes, sir, that's my name.   275

MISTRESS LOW-WATER.

    There should be a rank villain of that name;

    Came you out of that house?

SIR GILBERT.   How, sir slave!

MISTRESS LOW-WATER.

    Fall to your bull; leave roaring till anon.

WEATHERWISE.

    Yet again! and you love me gentlemen, let's have no

    roaring here. If I had thought that, I'd have sent my bull 280

    to the Bear Garden.

MASTER PEPPERTON.

    Why, so you should have wanted one of your signs.

WEATHERWISE.

    But I may chance want two now, and they fall together

    by the ears.

279–81.] Dyce; 2 metrical lines in
O, ending here./ garden.

---

271. *knave*] knight.
281. *Bear Garden*] famous bull-baiting pit.

LADY GOLDENFLEECE.

What's the strange fire that works in these two creatures? 285
Cold signs both, yet more hot than all their fellows.

WEATHERWISE.

Ho, Sol in Pisces! The sun's in New Fish Street. Here's
an end of this course.

PICKADILLE.

Madam, I am bold to remember your worship for a year's
wages and an livery cloak.   290

LADY GOLDENFLEECE.

How, will you shame me? Had you not both last week,
fool?

PICKADILLE.

Ay, but there's another year past since that.

LADY GOLDENFLEECE.

Would all your wit could make that good, sir.

PICKADILLE.

I am sure the sun has run through all the twelve signs 295
since, and that's a year; these gentlemen can witness.

WEATHERWISE.

The fool will live, madam.

PICKADILLE [aside].

Ay, as long as your eyes are open, I warrant him.

MISTRESS LOW-WATER.

Sirrah!

MASTER LOW-WATER.

Does your worship call?   300

MISTRESS LOW-WATER.

Commend my love and service to the widow;
Desire her ladyship to taste that morsel. [Gives him the letter.]

MASTER LOW-WATER [aside].

This is the bit I watch'd for all this while,
But it comes duly.

SIR GILBERT.

And wherein has this name of mine offended,   305

296. these] Bullen; this O.

---

286. Cold signs both] Taurus is cold and dry; Pisces is cold and
moist.

That y'are so liberal of your infamous titles?
I, but a stranger to thee; it must be known, sir,
Ere we two part.

MISTRESS LOW-WATER.   Marry, and reason, good sir.

LADY GOLDENFLEECE.

Oh, strike me cold! —This should be your hand, Sir
Gilbert?   310

SIR GILBERT.

Why, make you question of that madam? 'Tis one of the
letters I sent you.

LADY GOLDENFLEECE.

Much good do you, gentlemen.   [Rising.]

ALL.

How now? What's the matter?   [All rise.]

WEATHERWISE.

Look to the widow; she paints white; some *aqua coelistis* 315
for my lady! Run, villain!

PICKADILLE.

Aqua Solister! Can nobody help her case but a lawyer,
and so many suitors here?

LADY GOLDENFLEECE.

Oh, treachery unmatch'd, unheard of!

SIR GILBERT.

How do you, madam?   320

LADY GOLDENFLEECE.

Oh, impudence as foul! Does my disease
Ask how I do? Can it torment my heart,
And look with a fresh color in my face?

SIR GILBERT.

What's this? What's this?

WEATHERWISE.

I am sorry for this qualm, widow.   325

LADY GOLDENFLEECE.

He that would know a villain when he meets him,
Let him ne'er go to a conjurer; here's a glass
Will show him without money, and far truer.

---

315. *paints white*] turns pale.
315. *aqua coelistis*] a cordial.
327. *glass*] the letter.

Preserver of my state, pray tell me, sir,
That I may pay you all my thanks together,   330
What bless'd hap brought that letter to your hand
To free me, so fast lock'd in mine enemy's power?

MISTRESS LOW-WATER.

I will resolve you, madam. I have a kinsman
Somewhat infected with that wanton pity
Which men bestow on the distress of women,   335
Especially if they be fair and poor;
With such hot charity, which indeed is lust,
He sought t'entice, as his repentance told me,
Her whom you call your enemy, the wife
To a poor gentleman, one Low-water—   340

LADY GOLDENFLEECE.

Right, right, the same.

MASTER LOW-WATER [aside].

Had it been right, 't'ad now been.

MISTRESS LOW-WATER.

And, according to the common rate of sinners,
Offer'd large maintenance, which with her seem'd nothing;
For if she would consent, she told him roundly,   345
There was a knight had bid more at one minute
Than all his wealth could compass, and, withal,
Pluck'd out that letter as it were in scorn;
Which, by good fortune, he put up in jest
With promise that the writ should be returnable   350
The next hour of his meeting. But, sweet madam,
Out of my love and zeal, I did so practice
The part upon him of an urgent wooer
That neither he nor that return'd more to her.

SIR GILBERT [aside].

Plague o' that kinsman!

WEATHERWISE.   Here's a gallant rascal!   355

LADY GOLDENFLEECE.

Sir, you have appear'd so noble in this action,
So full of worth and goodness, that my thanks
Will rather shame the bounty of my mind
Than do it honor. —Oh, thou treacherous villain!

332. To free] this edn.; From O.

Does thy faith bear such fruit?   360
Are these the blossoms of a hundred oaths
Shot from thy bosom? Was thy love so spiteful
It could not be content to mock my heart,
Which is in love a misery too much,
But must extend so far to the quick ruin   365
Of what was painfully got, carefully left me;
And, 'mongst a world of yielding, needy women,
Choose no one to make merry with my sorrows,
And spend my wealth on, in adulterous surfeits,
But my most mortal enemy? Oh, despiteful!   370
Is this thy practice? Follow it, 'twill advance thee!
Go, beguile on! Have I so happily found
What many a widow has with sorrow tasted,
Even when my lip touch'd the contracting cup,
Even then to see the spider? 'Twas miraculous!   375
Crawl with thy poisons hence, and for thy sake
I'll never covet titles and more riches,
To fall into a gulf of hate and laughter.
I'll marry love hereafter; I've enough,
And wanting that, I have nothing. There's thy way.   380

MASTER OVERDON.
    Do you hear, sir? You must walk.

MASTER PEPPERTON.
    Hear't! Thrust him down stairs!

WEATHERWISE.
    Out of my house, you treacherous, lecherous rascal!

SIR GILBERT.
    All curses scatter you.   [*Exit.*]

WEATHERWISE.
    Life, do you thunder here! If you had stayed a little 385
    longer, I'd have ripp'd out some of my bull out of your
    belly again.

MASTER PEPPERTON.
    'Twas a most noble discovery; we must love you forever
    for't.

LADY GOLDENFLEECE.
    Sir, for your banquet and your mirth, we thank you;   390

You, gentlemen, for your kind company;
But, you, for all my merry days to come,
Or this had been the last else.
MISTRESS LOW-WATER.   Love and fortune
     Had more care of your safety, peace, and state, madam.
WEATHERWISE [*aside*].
     Now, will I thrust in for't.   395
MASTER PEPPERTON [*aside*].
     I'm for myself now.
MASTER OVERDON [*aside*].
     What's fifty years? 'Tis man's best time and season.
     Now the knight's gone, the widow will hear reason.
MASTER LOW-WATER.
     Now, now! The suitors flatter; hold on, Kate;
     The hen may pick the meat, while the cocks prate.   400
                                                        Exeunt.

[II.ii]
Enter Master Sandfield, Philip, *Sir Oliver Twilight's son, with*
Savorwit.

PHILIP.
     If thou talk'st longer, I shall turn to marble,
     And death will stop my hearing.
SANDFIELD.   Horrible fortune!
SAVORWIT.
     Nay, sir, our building is so far defac'd
     There is no stuff left to raise up a hope.
PHILIP.
     Oh, with more patience could my flesh endure   5
     A score of wounds and all their several searchings,
     Than this that thou hast told me.
SAVORWIT.   Would that Flemish ram
     Had ne'er come near our house! There's no going home
     As long as he has a nest there, and his young one,
     A little Flanders' egg new fledg'd; they gape   10
     For pork, and I shall be made meat for 'em.

398. knight's] *Dyce;* nights O.   II.ii] *Dyce; no scene division in O.*

_____

[II.ii]
   10. *fledg'd*] ready to fly.

PHILIP.

'Tis not the bare news of my mother's life—
May she live long and happy—that afflicts me
With half the violence that the latter draws,
Though in that news I have my share of grief,   15
As I had share of sin and a foul neglect;
It is my love's betraying; that's the sting
That strikes through flesh and spirit; and sense nor wit
From thee, in whom I ne'er saw ebb till now,
Nor comforts from a faithful friend can ease me.   20
I'll try the goodness of a third companion,
What he'll do for me.   [*Draws his sword.*]

SANDFIELD.   Hold! Why, friend?

SAVORWIT.

Why, master, is this all your kindness, sir? Offer to steal
into another country and ne'er take your leave on's?
Troth, I take it unkindly at your hands, sir; but I'll put   25
it up for once. [*Puts up the sword.*] Faith, there was no
conscience in this, sir: leave me here to endure all
weathers, whilst you make your soul dance like a juggler's
egg upon the point of a rapier! By my troth, sir, y'are too
blame in't; you might have given us an inkling of your   30
journey; perhaps others would as fain have gone as you.

PHILIP.

Burns this clay lamp of miserable life,
When joy, the oil that feeds it, is dried up?

Enter his mother [Lady Twilight] *new landed, with a gentleman*
[Master Beveril], *a scholar, and others.*

LADY TWILIGHT.

He has remov'd his house.

MASTER BEVERIL.   So it seems, madam.

LADY TWILIGHT.

I'll ask that gentleman. —Pray, can you tell me, sir,   35
Which is Sir Oliver Twilight's?

PHILIP.   Few can better, gentlewoman.
It is the next fair house your eye can fix on.

29–30. *too blame*] too much to blame; the "to" was misunderstood
as "too," and "blame" was considered an adjective *(OED).*

LADY TWILIGHT.

I thank you, sir. —Go on.—   [*Exeunt servants.*]

He had a son about some ten years since.

PHILIP.

That son still lives.

LADY TWILIGHT.   I pray, how does he, sir?   40

PHILIP [*aside*].

Faith, much about my health; that's never worse.—

If you have any business to him, gentlewoman,

I can cut short your journey to the house.

I'm all that ever was of the same kind.

LADY TWILIGHT.

Oh, my sweet son! Never fell fresher joy   45

Upon the heart of mother! —This is he, sir!

MASTER BEVERIL.

My seven-years' travel has ev'n worn him out

Of my remembrance.

SAVORWIT [*aside*].   Oh, this gear's worse and worse!

PHILIP.

I am so wonder struck at your bless'd presence

That through amaz'd joy, I neglect my duty.   [*Kneels.*] 50

LADY TWILIGHT.

Rise, and a thousand blessings spring up with thee!

SAVORWIT [*aside*].

I would we had but one in the mean time;

Let the rest grow at leisure.

LADY TWILIGHT.

But, know you not this gentleman yet, son?

PHILIP.

I take it's Master Beveril.

MASTER BEVERIL.   My name's Beveril, sir.   55

PHILIP.

Right welcome to my bosom!   [*Embracing* Beveril.]

LADY TWILIGHT.   You'd not think, son,

How much I am beholding to this gentleman,

As far as freedom; he laid out the ransom,

Finding me so distress'd.

55. I] *Dyce;* It *O.*

---

48. *gear*] affair.

PHILIP.   'Twas worthily done, sir,
     And I shall ever rest your servant for't.   60
MASTER BEVERIL.
     You quite forget your worth. 'Twas my good hap, sir,
     To return home that way after some travels;
     Where finding your good mother so distress'd,
     I could not but in pity see her releas'd.
PHILIP.
     It was a noble charity, sir; heaven quit you!   65
SAVORWIT [aside].
     It comes at last.
MASTER BEVERIL.   I left a sister here,
     New married when I last took leave of England.
PHILIP.
     Oh, Mistress Low-water.
MASTER BEVERIL.   Pray, sir, how does she?
PHILIP.
     So little comfort I can give you, sir,
     That I would fain excuse myself for silence.   70
MASTER BEVERIL.
     Why, what's the worst, sir?
PHILIP.   Wrongs has made her poor.
MASTER BEVERIL.
     You strike my heart! Alas, good gentlewoman!
PHILIP.
     Here's a gentleman; you know him; Master Sandfield.
MASTER BEVERIL.
     I crave pardon, sir.
PHILIP.
     He can resolve you from her kinswoman.   75
SANDFIELD.
     Welcome to England, madam.
LADY TWILIGHT.   Thanks, good sir.
PHILIP.
     Now there's no way to 'scape; I'm compass'd round;
     My shame is like a prisoner set with halberds.

73.] *this edn.; 2 lines in Q, end-*
ing Gentleman,/ Sandfield.

_____

75. *her kinswoman*] Jane.

SAVORWIT.

    Pish, master, master! 'Tis young flood again,
    And you can take your time now; away quick!   80

PHILIP.

    Push, thou'st a swimming head.

SAVORWIT.   Will you but hear me?

    When did you lose your tide when I set forth with you?

PHILIP.

    That's true.

SAVORWIT.   Regard me then; though you have no feeling,

    I would not hang by th' thumbs with a good will.

PHILIP.

    I hang by th' heart, sir, and would fain have ease.   85

SAVORWIT.

    Then this or none. Fly to your mother's pity,
    For that's the court must help you; y'are quite gone
    At common law, no counselor can hear you;
    Confess your follies and ask pardon for 'em.
    Tell her the state of all things; stand not nicely;   90
    The meat's too hard to be minc'd now;
    She breeds young bones by this time.
    Deal plainly; heaven will bless thee; turn out all,
    And shake your pockets after it. Beg, weep,
    Kneel, anything; 'twill break no bones, man.   95
    Let her not rest, take breathing time, nor leave thee
    Till thou hast got her help.

PHILIP.   Lad, I conceive thee.

SAVORWIT.

    About it then; it requires haste; do't well;
    There's but a short street between us and hell.

MASTER BEVERIL.

    Ah, my poor sister!

LADY TWILIGHT.   'Las, good gentlewoman!   100

    My heart ev'n weeps for her. —Ay, son, we'll go now.

PHILIP.

    May I crave one word, madam?   *Shogs his mother.*

---

102. *S.D. Shogs*] jogs to attract attention.

LADY TWILIGHT.   With me, son?
     The more, the better welcome.
SAVORWIT [*aside*].   Now, now luck!
     I pray not often, the last prayer I made
     Was nine-year-old last Bartholomew-tide; 'twould have 105
       been
     A jolly chopper, and 't'ad liv'd till this time.
LADY TWILIGHT.
     Why do your words start back? Are they afraid
     Of her that ever lov'd them?
PHILIP.   I have a suit to you, madam.
LADY TWILIGHT.
     You have told me that already; pray what is't?
     If't be so great, my present state refuse it,   110
     I shall be abler, then command and use it;
     Whate'er 't be, let me have warning to provide for't.
PHILIP [*kneels*].
     Provide forgiveness then, for that's the want
     My conscience feels. Oh, my wild youth has led me
     Into unnatural wrongs against your freedom once.   115
     I spent the ransom which my father sent,
     To set my pleasures free, while you lay captive.
SAVORWIT [*aside*].
     He does it finely, faith.
LADY TWILIGHT.   And is this all now?
     You use me like a stranger; pray stand up.
PHILIP.
     Rather fall flat; I shall deserve yet worse.   120
LADY TWILIGHT [*raising* Philip].
     Whate'er your faults are, esteem me still a friend,
     Or else you wrong me more in asking pardon
     Than when you did the wrong you ask'd it for,
     And since you have prepar'd me to forgive you,
     Pray let me know for what; the first fault's nothing. 125

105–6.] *Dyce; in O lines end*
Tide; / time.

_____

     105. *Bartholomew-tide*] The day or tide of St. Bartholomew is 24
August.

SAVORWIT [*aside*].

    'Tis a sweet lady, every inch of her.

PHILIP.

    Here comes the wrong then that drives home the rest.
    I saw a face at Antwerp that quite drew me
    From conscience and obedience; in that fray
    I lost my heart; I must needs lose my way;   130
    There went the ransom, to redeem my mind;
    'Stead of the money, I brought over her;
    And to cast mists before my father's eyes,
    Told him it was my sister, lost so long,
    And that yourself was dead. You see the wrong?   135

LADY TWILIGHT.

    This is but youthful still. Oh, that word "sister"
    Afflicts me when I think on't. I forgive thee
    As freely as thou didst it. For, alas,
    This may be call'd good dealing to some parts,
    That love and youth plays daily among sons.   140

SAVORWIT [*aside*].

    She helps our knavery well; that's one good comfort.

PHILIP.

    But such is the hard plight my state lives in
    That 'twixt forgiveness, I must sin again,
    And seek my help where I bestow'd my wrongs.
    Oh, mother, pity once, though against reason,   145
    'Cause I can merit none; though my wrongs grieve you,
    Yet let it be your glory to relieve me.

LADY TWILIGHT.

    Wherein have I given cause yet of mistrust,
    That you should doubt my succor and my love?
    Show me but in what kind I may bestow 'em.   150

PHILIP.

    There came a Dutchman with report this day
    That you were living.

LADY TWILIGHT.   Came he so lately?

PHILIP.   Yes, madam.

    Which news so struck my father on the sudden
    That he grows jealous of my faith in both.

---

154. *jealous*] suspicious.

These five hours have I kept me from his sight 155
And wish'd myself eternally so hid;
And surely, had not your bless'd presence quicken'd
The flame of life in me, all had gone out.
Now to confirm me to his trust again,
And settle much aright in his opinion, 160
Say but she is my sister, and all's well.

LADY TWILIGHT.

You ask devotion like a bashful beggar
That pure need urges, and not lazy impudence;
And to express how glad I am to pity you,
My bounty shall flow over your demand. 165
I will not only with a constant breath
Approve that, but excuse thee for my death.

SAVORWIT [aside].

Why, here's a woman made as a man would wish to have her.

PHILIP.

Oh, I am plac'd higher in happiness
Than whence I fell before! 170

SAVORWIT [aside].

We're brave fellows once again, and we can keep our own.
Now, hoffte toffte, our pipes play as loftily!

MASTER BEVERIL.

My sister fled!

SANDFIELD.

Both fled; that's the news now. Want must obey;
Oppressions came so thick, they could not stay. 175

MASTER BEVERIL.

Mean are my fortunes, yet had I been nigh,
Distress nor wrong should have made virtue fly.

LADY TWILIGHT.

Spoke like a brother, worthy such a sister.

MASTER BEVERIL.

Grief's like a new wound; heat beguiles the sense,
For I shall feel this smart more three days hence. 180
Come, madam, sorrow's rude and forgets manners.

[Exeunt all except Savorwit.]

---

167. *Approve*] confirm.

SAVORWIT.

Our knavery is for all the world like a shifting bankrupt;
it breaks in one place, and sets up in another; he tries
all trades, from a goldsmith to a tobacco seller; we try
all shifts, from an outlaw to a flatterer; he cozens the 185
husband, and compounds with the widow; we cozen my
master, and compound with my mistress; only here I turn
o'th' right hand from him; he is known to live like a
rascal, when I am thought to live like a gentleman.   *Exit.*

[II.iii]
Enter Kate [Mistress Low-water] *with her man-husband* [Master
Low-water, *both disguised as before*].

MISTRESS LOW-WATER.

I have sent in one to th' widow.

MASTER LOW-WATER.   Well said, Kate,

Thou ply'st thy business close. The coast is clear yet.

MISTRESS LOW-WATER.

Let me but have warning,
I shall make pretty shift with them.

MASTER LOW-WATER.

That thou shalt, wench.   *Exit.*   5

[*Enter* Servant.]

SERVANT.

My lady, sir, commends her kindly to you,
And for the third part of an hour, sir,
Desires your patience.
Two or three of her tenants out of Kent
Will hold her so long busied.

MISTRESS LOW-WATER.   Thank you, sir.   10

'Tis fit I should attend her time and leisure.   [*Exit* Servant.]
Those were my tenants once, but what relief

189.S.D.] *Dyce; Exeunt O.*   II.iii.] *Dyce; no scene division in
O.*

[II.iii]
2. *ply'st*] to work vigorously.
4. *make pretty shift*] contrive goals.

Is there in what hath been, or what I was?
'Tis now that makes the man. A last year's feast
Yields little comfort for the present humor;   15
He starves that feeds his hopes with what is past.—

[*Enter* Master Low-water.]

How now?

MASTER LOW-WATER.
They're come, newly alighted.

MISTRESS LOW-WATER.   Peace, peace!
I'll have a trick for 'em; look you second me well now.

MASTER LOW-WATER.
I warrant thee.

MISTRESS LOW-WATER. I must seem very imperious, I can tell
you;   20
Therefore, if I should chance to use you roughly,
Pray, forgive me beforehand.

MASTER LOW-WATER.   With all my heart, Kate.

MISTRESS LOW-WATER.
You must look for no obedience in these clothes;
That lies in the pocket of my gown.

MASTER LOW-WATER.
Well, well, I will not then.   25

MISTRESS LOW-WATER.
I hear 'em coming; step back a little, sir.—

Enter Master Weatherwise, Master Pepperton, *and* Master Overdon, *suitors.*

Where be those fellows? Who looks out there? Is there
ne'er a knave i'th' house to take those gentlemen's horses?
Where wait you today? How stand you like a dreaming
goose in a corner, the gentlemen's horses, forsooth!   30

MASTER LOW-WATER.
Yes, an't like your worship.   [*Exit.*]

MASTER PEPPERTON.
What's here? A strange alteration!

16. is] *Dyce;* his *O.*   23. these] *Dyce;* those *O.*
                                       26.1.]*before l. 32 in O.*

---

23. *these clothes*] her disguise.

WEATHERWISE.

 A new lord? Would I were upon my mare's back again
then,

MISTRESS LOW-WATER.

 Pray, gentlemen, pardon the rudeness of these grooms; 35
I hope they will be brought to better fashion.

 In the meantime, y'are welcome, gentlemen.

ALL.

 We thank you, sir.

WEATHERWISE [aside].

 Life, here's quick work! [Taking out almanac.] I'll hold
my life h'as struck the widow i'th' right planet. Venus in 40
cauda! I thought 'twas a lecherous planet that goes to't
with a caudle.

    [Enter Master Low-water.]

MISTRESS LOW-WATER.

 How now, sir?

MASTER LOW-WATER.

 The gentlemen's horses are set up, sir.

MASTER PEPPERTON.

 No, no, no, we'll away!   45

WEATHERWISE.

 We'll away.

MISTRESS LOW-WATER.

 How! By my faith, but you shall not yet, by your leave!
Where's Bess? Call your mistress, sir, to welcome these
kind gentlemen, my friends.   [Exit Master Low-water.]

MASTER PEPPERTON.

 How! Bess?   50

MASTER OVERDON.

 Peg?

50–51.] Dyce; Peppert. Overd.
How Bess, Peg? O.

 40–41. Venus in cauda] the planet Venus in the Dragon's tail (Latin,
cauda), which is the descending node of the moon's orbit with the
ecliptic. When a planet is joined with the Dragon's tail, the malevolent
aspects of that planet are "doubled and trebeled, or extreamely aug-
mented"; for Venus, it means increased lewdness and lechery (Lilly,
Christian Astrology, p. 74, p. 83).

 42. caudle] a warm spiced drink used as an aphrodisiac.

WEATHERWISE.

Plain Bess! I know how the world goes then; he has been
a-bed with Bess, i'faith; there's no trust to these widows;
a young horsing gentleman carries 'em away clear.

[*Enter* Master Low-water.]

MISTRESS LOW-WATER.

Now, where's your mistress, sir; how chance she comes not?   55

MASTER LOW-WATER.

Sir, she requests you to excuse her for a while; she's busy
with a milliner about gloves.

MISTRESS LOW-WATER.

Gloves?

WEATHERWISE.

Hoyda! Gloves, too!

MISTRESS LOW-WATER.

Could she find no other time to choose gloves but now   60
when my friends are here?

MASTER PEPPERTON.

No, sir, 'tis no matter; we thank you for your good will,
sir; to say truth, we have no business with her at all at
this time, i'faith, sir.

MISTRESS LOW-WATER.

Oh, that's another matter: yet, stay, stay, gentlemen, and   65
taste a cup of wine ere you go.

MASTER OVERDON.

No, thank you, sir.

MISTRESS LOW-WATER.

Master Pepperton, Master Weatherwise, will you, sir?

WEATHERWISE.

I'll see the wine in a drunkard's shoes first, and drink't
after he has brew'd it; but let her go; she's fitted, i'faith;   70
a proud surly sir here, he domineers already; one that
will shake her bones, and go to dice with her money, or
I have no skill in a calendar. Life! He that can be so

---

52. *Plain Bess*] Custom forbade affectionate diminutives before marriage.

59. *Gloves*] customary gifts of the bride to the groom's men (Brand,
p. 369). See Ben Jonson's *Epicoene*, III.vi.70–72.

saucy to call her Bess already, will call her prating-quean
a month hence.   *Exeunt [suitors].*   75
MASTER LOW-WATER.
    They have given thee all the slip.
MISTRESS LOW-WATER.   So, a fair riddance.
    There's three rubs gone; I've a clear way to th'mistress.
MASTER LOW-WATER.
    You'd need have a clear way, because y'are a bad pricker.
MISTRESS LOW-WATER.
    Yet if my bowl take bank, I shall go nigh
    To make myself a saver;   80
    Here's alley room enough; I'll try my fortune.
    I am to begin the world like a younger brother;
    I know that a bold face and a good spirit
    Is all the jointure he can make a widow.
    An't shall go hard, but I'll be as rich as he,   85
    Or at least seem so, and that's wealth enough;
    For nothing kills a widow's heart so much
    As a faint bashful wooer; though he have thousands,
    And come with a poor water-gruel spirit
    And a fish-market face, he shall ne'er speed.   90
    I would not have himself left a poor widower.
MASTER LOW-WATER.
    Faith, I'm glad I'm alive to commend thee, Kate. I shall
    be sure now to see my commendations delivered.
MISTRESS LOW-WATER.
    I'll put her to't, i'faith.
MASTER LOW-WATER.   But soft ye, Kate.
    How and she should accept of your bold kindness?   95
MISTRESS LOW-WATER.
    A chief point to be thought on, by my faith.

84. a] *Dyce; not in O.*

---

74. *prating-quean*] chattering whore.
77. *three rubs . . . mistress*] In the game of lawn bowling, the *mistress*
or jack was the small *bowl* or ball which served as the target. A *rub*
was an impediment or tuft in the turf which would cause the bowled
ball to go awry; the open greens were not perfectly flat and a skilled
bowler took advantage of the *banks* or the *alley* in casting the bowl
(Cotton).

Marry, therefore, sir, be you sure to step in,
For fear I should shame myself and spoil all.

MASTER LOW-WATER.

Well, I'll save your credit then for once,
But look you come there no more.   100

MISTRESS LOW-WATER.

Away, I hear her coming.

MASTER LOW-WATER.   I am vanish'd.   *Exit.*

Enter Widow [Lady Goldenfleece].

MISTRESS LOW-WATER.

How does my life, my soul, my dear sweet madam?

LADY GOLDENFLEECE.

I have wrong'd your patience; made you stand too long
here.

MISTRESS LOW-WATER.

There's no such thing, i'faith, madam; y'are pleas'd to 105
say so.

LADY GOLDENFLEECE.

Yes, I confess I was too slow, sir.

MISTRESS LOW-WATER.

Why, you shall make me amends for that then, with a
quickness in your bed.

LADY GOLDENFLEECE.

That were a speedy mends, sir.   110

MISTRESS LOW-WATER.

Why, then you are out of my debt; I'll cross the book,
and turn over a new leaf with you.

LADY GOLDENFLEECE.

So, with paying a small debt, I may chance run into a
greater.

MISTRESS LOW-WATER.

My faith, your credit will be the better then. There's 115
many a brave gallant would be glad of such fortune, and
pay use for't.

---

117. *use*] interest.

LADY GOLDENFLEECE.

Some of them have nothing else to do; they would be idle
and 'twere not for interest.

MISTRESS LOW-WATER.

I promise you, widow, were I a setter-up, such is my opin-   120
ion of your payment, I durst trust you with all the ware
in my shop.

LADY GOLDENFLEECE.

I thank you for your good will; I can have no more.

MISTRESS LOW-WATER [aside].

Not of me, i'faith, nor that neither, and you know all.
—Come make but short service, widow, a kiss and to bed,   125
I'm very hungry, i'faith, wench.

LADY GOLDENFLEECE.

What are you, sir?

MISTRESS LOW-WATER.

Oh, a younger brother has an excellent stomach, madam,
worth a hundred of your sons and heirs that stay their
wedding stomachs with a hot bit of a common mistress,   130
and then come to a widow's bed like a flash of lightning.
Y'are sure of the first of me, not of the five hundredth of
them. I never took physic yet in my life; you shall have
the doctor continually with them, or some bottle for
his deputy; out flies your moneys for restoratives and   135
strength'nings; in me 'tis sav'd in your purse, and found
in your children; they'll get peevish pothecaries' stuff, you
may weigh 'em by th'ounces; I, boys of war, brave com-
manders, that shall bear a breadth in their shoulders and
a weight in their hips, and run over a whole country with   140
a pound o' beef and a biscuit in their belly. Ho, widow,
my kisses are virgins, my embraces perfect, my strength
solid, my love constant, my heat comfortable; but to come
to the point, inutterable—

LADY GOLDENFLEECE.

But soft ye, soft ye; because you stand so strictly   145
Upon your purity, I'll put you to't, sir.
Will you swear here, you never yet knew woman?

---

120. *setter-up*] a beginner in business.

MISTRESS LOW-WATER.
　　Never, as man e'er knew her, by this light, widow.
LADY GOLDENFLEECE.
　　What, what, sir? —[*Aside.*] 'Shrew my heart, he moves me
　　much.   150
MISTRESS LOW-WATER.
　　Nay, since you love to bring a man on's knees,
　　I take into the same oath thus much more,
　　That y'are the first widow, or maid, or wife
　　That ever I in suit of love did court
　　Or honestly did woo. How say you to that, widow?   155
LADY GOLDENFLEECE.
　　Marry, I say, sir, you had a good portion of chastity left
　　you, though ill fortune run away with the rest.
MISTRESS LOW-WATER.
　　That I kept for thee, widow; she's of fortune, and all her
　　strait-bodied daughters; thou shalt have't, widow. [*Kisses her.*]
LADY GOLDENFLEECE.
　　Push, what do you mean?   160
MISTRESS LOW-WATER.
　　I cannot bestow't better.
LADY GOLDENFLEECE.
　　I'll call my servants.
MISTRESS LOW-WATER.
　　By my troth, you shall not, madam.

Enter Master Low-water.

MASTER LOW-WATER.
　　Does your worship call, sir?
MISTRESS LOW-WATER.
　　Ha, pox! Are you peeping?—   165
　　　　　　　　Throws somewhat at him [*who exits*].
　　[*Aside.*] He came in a good time, I thank him for't.
LADY GOLDENFLEECE.
　　What do you think of me? You're very forward, sir.
MISTRESS LOW-WATER.
　　Extremity of love.
LADY GOLDENFLEECE.   You say y'are ignorant,
　　It should not seem so surely by your play;

— 68 —

For aught I see, you may make one yourself;   170
You need not hold the cards to any gamester.

MISTRESS LOW-WATER.

That love should teach men ways to wrong itself!

LADY GOLDENFLEECE.

Are these the first fruits of your boldness, sir?
If all take after these, you may boast on 'em.
There comes few such to market among women;   175
Time you were taken down, sir. —Within, there!

MISTRESS LOW-WATER [aside].

I've lost my way again.
There's but two paths that lead to widows' beds,
That's wealth or forwardness, and I've took the wrong
    one.

Enter Servant, *with the suitors* [Weatherwise, Master Pepperton,
and Master Overdon].

SERVANT.

He marry my lady? Why, there's no such thought yet. 180
                                                    [*Exit.*]

MISTRESS LOW-WATER [aside].

Oh, here they are all again, too.

LADY GOLDENFLEECE.

Are you come, gentlemen? I wish no better men.

WEATHERWISE.

Oh, the moon's chang'd now!

LADY GOLDENFLEECE.

See you that gentleman yonder?

MASTER PEPPERTON.

Yes, sweet madam.   185

LADY GOLDENFLEECE.

Then pray be witness all of you; with this kiss
                            [*Kisses* Mistress Low-water.]
I choose him for my husband.

ALL SUITORS.

A pox on't.

182.] *this edn.; 2 lines in O, ending* Gentlemen?/ men.

LADY GOLDENFLEECE.

And with this parted gold, that two hearts join.

[*Breaks a piece of gold and gives half to* Mistress Low-water.]

MISTRESS LOW-WATER.

Never with chaster love than this of mine.   190

LADY GOLDENFLEECE.

And those that have the hearts to come to th' wedding,
They shall be welcome for their former loves.   *Exit.*

MASTER PEPPERTON.

No, I thank you; y'ave chok'd me already.

WEATHERWISE.

I never suspected mine almanac 'till now. I believe he
plays cogging John with me; I bought it at his shop; it 195
may learn the more knavery by that.

MISTRESS LOW-WATER.

Now indeed, gentlemen, I can bid you welcome;
Before 'twas but a flourish.

WEATHERWISE.

Nay, so my almanac told me there should be an eclipse,
but not visible in our horizon, but about the western 200
inhabitants of Mexicana and California.

MISTRESS LOW-WATER.

Well, we have no business there, sir.

WEATHERWISE.

Nor we have none here, sir, and so fare you well.

                                    [*Exeunt Suitors.*]

MISTRESS LOW-WATER.

You save the house a good labor, gentlemen; the fool
carries them away in a voider. —Where be these fellows? 205

Enter Servant[, *with* Master Low-water *and* Pickadille].

SERVANT.

Sir?

203.1] *this edn.; Exit* O.   205.1. Servant] *Dyce; Servants* O.

---

189. *parted gold*] Parted gold and a public kiss are betrothal customs.
195. *cogging*] cheating.
199. *an eclipse*] a portent of disaster, even if it occurred in remote
and barbaric places. 205. *voider*] a tray or basket for clearing a table.

PICKADILLE.
　Here, sir.

SERVANT.
　What's your worship's pleasure?

MISTRESS LOW-WATER.
　Oh, this is something like. —Take you your ease, sir;
　Here are those now more fit to be commanded.　　210

MASTER LOW-WATER [aside].
　How few women are of thy mind; she thinks it too much
　to keep me in subjection for one day, whereas some wives
　would be glad to keep their husbands in awe all days of
　their lives and think it the best bargain that e'er they
　made.　　　　　　　　　　　　　　　[Exit.] 215

MISTRESS LOW-WATER.
　I'll spare no cost for th' wedding, some device too,
　To show our thankfulness to wit and fortune;
　It shall be so. —Run straight for one o'th' wits.

PICKADILLE.
　How, one o'th' wits? I care not if I run on that account;
　are they in town think you?　　　　　　　　　220

MISTRESS LOW-WATER.
　Whither runn'st thou now?

PICKADILLE.
　To an ordinary for one of the wits.

MISTRESS LOW-WATER.
　Why to an ordinary, above a tavern?

PICKADILLE.
　No, I hold your best wits to be at ordinary, nothing so
　good in a tavern.　　　　　　　　　　　225

MISTRESS LOW-WATER.
　And why I pray, sir?

PICKADILLE.
　Because those that go to an ordinary dine better for

208. What's your worship's] Dyce;
What your worship O.

---

　209. something like] as it should be.
　216. device] an entertainment.
　223. ordinary] an eating house or restaurant; a tavern was primarily
a drinking, not eating, establishment.

twelve pence than he that goes to a tavern for his five
shillings, and I think those have the best wits that can
save four shillings, and fare better too.   230

MISTRESS LOW-WATER.
So, sir, all your wit then runs upon victuals.

PICKADILLE.
'Tis a sign 'twill hold out the longer then.

MISTRESS LOW-WATER.
What were you saying to me?

SERVANT.   Please, your worship,
I heard there came a scholar over lately
With old Sir Oliver's lady.

MISTRESS LOW-WATER [aside].   Is she come?—   235
What is that lady?

SERVANT.   A good gentlewoman,
Has been long prisoner with the enemy.

MISTRESS LOW-WATER [aside].
I know't too well, and joy in her release.—
Go to that house then straight, and in one labor
You may bid them, and entreat home that scholar.   240

SERVANT.
It shall be done with speed, sir.   [Exit.]

PICKADILLE.   I'll along with you,
And see what face that scholar has brought over;
A thin pair of parbreaking sea-water green chops,
I warrant you.   [Exit.]

MISTRESS LOW-WATER.
Since wit has pleasur'd me, I'll pleasure wit;   245
Scholars shall fare the better. Oh, my blessing!
I feel a hand of mercy lift me up
Out of a world of waters, and now sets me
Upon a mountain, where the sun plays most,
To cheer my heart ev'n as it dries my limbs.   250

241–44. I'll . . . you] this edn.; in   243. parbreaking] Dyce; Barbreak-
O lines end you/ over;/ Green-/   ing O.
you.

---

243. parbreaking] vomiting.
245–62.] one of the play's few extended passages of poetry; it is
reminiscent of The Second Maiden's Tragedy, V.ii.2422–25.

What deeps I see beneath me, in whose falls
Many a nimble mortal toils,
And scarce can feed himself! The streams of fortune
'Gainst which he tugs in vain, still beat him down,
And will not suffer him, past hand to mouth,   255
To lift his arm to his posterity's blessing.
I see a careful sweat run in a ring
About his temples, but all will not do,
For till some happy means relieve his state,
There he must stick and bide the wrath of fate!   260
I see this wrath upon an uphill land;
Oh, bless'd are they can see their falls, and stand!

                    Enter [Servant *with*] Beveril.

How now?
SERVANT.
        With much entreating, sir; he's come.   [*Exit.*]
MISTRESS LOW-WATER.
        Sir y'are—[*aside*] my brother! Joys come thick together!— 265
                                    [*Embracing him.*]
        Sir, when I see a scholar, pardon me,
        I am so taken with affection for him
        That I must run into his arms and clasp him.
MASTER BEVERIL.
        Art stands in need, sir, of such cherishers;
        I meet too few; 'twere a brave world for scholars   270
        If half a kingdom were but of your mind, sir;
        Let ignorance and hell confound the rest.
MISTRESS LOW-WATER.
        Let it suffice, sweet sir; you cannot think
        How dearly you are welcome.
MASTER BEVERIL.   May I live
        To show you service for't.
MISTRESS LOW-WATER.   Your love, your love, sir,   275
        We go no higher, nor shall you go lower.
        Sir, I'm bold to send for you, to request
        A kindness from your wit, for some device

262.1] *after l. 263 in* O.   273. suffice] *Dyce;* suffer O.
267. affection] *Dyce;* affliction O.

> To grace our wedding; it shall be worth your pains,
> And something more t'express my love to art;   280
> You shall not receive all in bare embracements.

MASTER BEVERIL.

> Your love I thank, but pray, sir, pardon me,
> I've a heart says I must not grant you that.

MISTRESS LOW-WATER.

> No, what's your reason, sir?

MASTER BEVERIL.   I'm not at peace

> With the lady of this house; now you'll excuse me;   285
> Sh'as wrong'd my sister, and I may not do't.

MISTRESS LOW-WATER.

> The widow knows you not.

MASTER BEVERIL.

> I never saw her face to my remembrance.
> Oh, that my heart should feel her wrongs so much,
> And yet live ignorant of the injurer!   290

MISTRESS LOW-WATER.

> Let me persuade thee, since she knows you not,
> Make clear the weather; let not griefs betray you;
> I'll tell her y'are a worthy friend of mine,
> And so I tell her true, thou art indeed.
> Sir, here she comes.

Enter Widow [Lady Goldenfleece].

LADY GOLDENFLEECE.   What, are you busy, sir?   295

MISTRESS LOW-WATER.

> Nothing less, lady; here's a gentleman
> Of noble parts, beside his friendship to me;
> Pray, give him liberal welcome.

LADY GOLDENFLEECE.   He's most welcome.

MISTRESS LOW-WATER.

> The virtues of his mind will deserve largely.

LADY GOLDENFLEECE [*aside*].

> Methinks his outward parts deserve as much then; 300
> A proper gentleman it is.

MISTRESS LOW-WATER.   Come, worthy sir.

MASTER BEVERIL.

    I follow.   [*Exeunt all but* Master Beveril.]
        Check thy blood.
    For fear it prove too bold to wrong thy goodness.
    A wise man makes affections but his slaves;
    Break 'em in time, let 'em not master thee.   305
    Oh, 'tis my sister's enemy, think of that!
    Some speedy grief fall down upon the fire,
    Before it take my heart; let it not rise
    'Gainst brotherly nature, judgment, and these wrongs.
    Make clear the weather!   310
    Oh, who could look upon her face in storms!
    Yet pains may work it out; griefs do but strive
    To kill this spark; I'll keep it still alive.   [*Exit.*]

[III.i]
Enter the three late suitors, Weatherwise, Pepperton, *and* Overdon, *join'd with* Sir Gilbert Lambston.

WEATHERWISE.

    Faith, Sir Gilbert, forget and forgive;
    There's all our hands to a new bargain of friendship.

MASTER PEPPERTON.

    Ay, and all our hearts to boot, Sir Gilbert.

WEATHERWISE.

    Why, la, you! There's but four suitors left on's in all th'
    world, and the fifth has the widow; if we should not be   5
    kind to one another, and so few on's, i'faith, I would we
    were all rak'd up in some hole or other.

SIR GILBERT.

    Pardon me, gentlemen, I cannot but remember
    Your late disgraceful words before the widow,
    In time of my oppression.   10

WEATHERWISE.

    Puh, Saturn reign'd then, a melancholy, grumbling

[III.i]
11–12. *Saturn . . . third house*] When Saturn is in the third house,
Mercury is the Lord of the Ascendant and Saturn is in opposition to
Mercury, resulting in an "ill dignified" Saturn, who becomes "envious,
covetous, jealous and mistrustful," leading to contention and trouble
(Lilly, *Christian Astrology*, p. 58).

planet; he was in the third house of privy enemies, and
would have bewray'd all our plots; beside there was a
fiery conjunction in the dragon's tail that spoil'd all that
e'er we went about.   15

SIR GILBERT.

Dragon or devil, somewhat 'twas I am sure.

WEATHERWISE.

Why, I tell you, Sir Gilbert, we were all out of our wits
in't; I was so mad at that time myself, I could have
wish'd an hind-quarter of my bull out of your belly
again, whereas now I care not if you had eat tail and all;   20
I am no niggard in the way of friendship; I was ever yet
at full moon in good fellowship, and so you shall find,
if you look into the almanac of my true nature.

SIR GILBERT.

Well, all's forgiven for once; hands apace, gentlemen.

WEATHERWISE.

Ye shall have two of mine to do you a kindness; yet,   25
when they're both abroad, who shall look to th' house
here?   [*Clasps hands with* Sir Gilbert.]

PEPPERTON. OVERDON.

Not only a new friendship, but a friend.
                                       [*Clasp hands with* Sir Gilbert.]

SIR GILBERT.

But upon this condition, gentlemen,
You shall hear now a thing worth your revenge.   30

WEATHERWISE.

And you doubt that,
You shall have mine beforehand; I've one ready;
I never go without a black oath about me.

SIR GILBERT.

I know the least touch of a spur in this

14. tail] *Dyce;* tails Q.   32–33.] *Dyce; in* O *lines end* I/
                                        me.

---

14. *fiery conjunction . . . tail*] A comet, a bad omen, conjoined
with the Dragon's tail must have been the height of evil influence.

Will now put your desires to a false gallop,   35
By all means sland'rous in every place,
And in all companies, to disgrace the widow,
No matter in what rank, so it be spiteful
And worthy your revenges; so now I;
It shall be all my study, care, and pains,   40
And we can lose no labor; all her foes
Will make such use on't that they'll snatch it from us
Faster than we can forge it, though we keep
Four tongues at work upon't and never cease.
Then for the indifferent world, faith, they're apter   45
To bid a slander welcome than a truth;
We have the odds of our side; this in time
May grow so general, as disgrace will spread,
That wild dissension may divide the bed.

WEATHERWISE. PEPPERTON.

Excellent!   50

MASTER OVERDON.

A pure revenge; I see no dregs in't.

SIR GILBERT.

Let each man look to his part now, and not feed
Upon one dish all four on's, like plain maltmen;
For at this feast we must have several kickshaws,
And delicate made dishes, that the world   55
May see it is a banquet finely furnish'd.

WEATHERWISE.

Why, then let me alone for one of your kickshaws;
I have thought on that already.

SIR GILBERT.   Prithee, how, sir?

WEATHERWISE.

Marry, sir, I'll give it out abroad that I have lain with
the widow myself, as 'tis the fashion of many a gallant to   60
disgrace his new mistress when he cannot have his will of
her, and lie with her name in every tavern, though he
ne'er came within a yard of her person; so I, being a

46. slander] *Dyce;* slave *O.*

_____

53. *maltmen*] brewers.
54. *kickshaws*] elaborately made dishes of food.

gentleman, may say as much in that kind as a gallant;
I am as free by my father's copy.   65

SIR GILBERT.

This will do excellent, sir.

WEATHERWISE.

And moreover, I'll give the world thus much to understand beside, that if I had not lain with the widow in the
wane of the moon, at one of my Seven Stars' houses,
when Venus was about business of her own and could   70
give no attendance, she had been brought a-bed with two
roaring boys by this time, and the Gemini being infants,
I'd have made away with them like a stepmother, and put
mine own boys in their places.

SIR GILBERT.

Why, this is beyond talk; you out-run your master.   75

Enter clown [Pickadille].

PICKADILLE [*aside*].

Whoop! Draw home next time; here are all the old shooters that have lost the game at pricks! What a fair mark
had Sir Gilbert on't, if he had shot home before the last
arrow came in. Methinks these show to me now, for all
the world, like so many lousy beggars turn'd out of my   80
lady's barn, and have ne'er a hole to put their heads in.

WEATHERWISE.

Mass, here's her ladyship's ass; he tells us anything.

SIR GILBERT.

Ho, Pickadille!

PICKADILLE.

What, Sir Gilbert Lambston!
Gentlemen, outlaws all, how do you do?   85

SIR GILBERT.

How! What do'st call us? How goes the world at home,
     lad?
What strange news?

PICKADILLE.

This is the state of prodigals as right as can be; when

---

77. *game at pricks*] one form of archery in which the targets, or
pricks, had a bull's eye in the center; a pun on *shooters.*

they have spent all their means on brave feasts, they're
glad to scrape to a servingman for a meal's meat.   90
So you that whilom, like four prodigal rivals,
Could goose or capon, crane or woodcock choose,
Now're glad to make up a poor meal with news;
A lamentable hearing!

WEATHERWISE.

He's in passion, up to the eyebrows for us.   95

PICKADILLE.

Oh, Master Weatherwise, I blame none but you.
You are a gentleman deeply read in Pond's Almanac;
Methinks you should not be such a shallow fellow;
You knew this day, the twelfth of June, would come
When the sun enters into the Crab's room,   100
And all your hopes would go aside, aside.

WEATHERWISE.

The fool says true, i'faith, gentlemen. I knew
'Twould come all to this pass; I'll show't you presently.
                              [*Takes out almanac.*]

PICKADILLE.

If you had spar'd but four of your twelve signs now,
You might have gone to a tavern and made merry with
  'em.   105

WEATHERWISE.

H'as the best moral meaning of an ass that e'er I heard
speak with tongue—look you here, gentlemen— [*Reading
almanac.*] "Fifth day, neither fish nor flesh."

PICKADILLE.

No, nor good red herring, and you look again.

---

89. they're] *Dyce;* their *O.*   102–3.] *this edn.; prose in O.*
96–101.] *Dyce; prose in O.*

---

91. *whilom*] formerly.
97. *Pond's Almanac*] Edward Pond began publishing almanacs in
1601; his annual publications were continuous from 1604–1709 *(DNB).*
The almanac poesies, however, are recited by Weatherwise from Thomas
Bretnor's 1611 almanac; see "Dating and Authorship" in Introduction,
above.
99. *the twelfth of June*] summer solstice, according to the old style
calendar, when the sun entered the house of Cancer the Crab.

WEATHERWISE [*reading*].
    "Sixth day, privily prevented."   110
PICKADILLE.
    Marry, faugh!
WEATHERWISE [*reading*].
    "Seventh day, shrunk in the wetting."
PICKADILLE.
    Nay, so will the best ware bought for love or money.
WEATHERWISE [*reading*].
    "The eighth day, over head and ears."
PICKADILLE.
    By my faith, he come home in a sweet pickle then.   115
WEATHERWISE [*reading*].
    "The ninth day, scarce sound at heart."
PICKADILLE.
    What o' pox ail'd it?
WEATHERWISE [*reading*].
    "The tenth day, a courtier's welcome."
PICKADILLE.
    That's a cup of beer, and you can get it.
WEATHERWISE [*reading*].
    "The eleventh day, stones against the wind."   120
PICKADILLE.
    Pox of an ass! He might have thrown 'em better.   ·
WEATHERWISE.
    Now the twelfth day, gentlemen, that was our day—
    [*reads*] "Past all redemption."
PICKADILLE.
    Then the devil go with't.
WEATHERWISE.
    Now you see plainly, gentlemen, how we're us'd,   125
    The calendar will not lie for no man's pleasure.
SIR GILBERT.
    Push, y'are too confident in almanac posies.
MASTER PEPPERTON.
    Faith, so said we.
SIR GILBERT.
    They're mere delusions.

---

110. *privily*] privately, but Pickadille puns on it.

WEATHERWISE.

How! You see how knavishly they happen, sir.   130

SIR GILBERT.

Ay, that's because they're foolishly believ'd, sir.

WEATHERWISE.

Well, take your courses, gentlemen, without 'em, and see
what will come on't; you may wander like masterless
men; there's ne'er a planet will care a half-penny for you.
If they look after you, I'll be hang'd, when you scorn to 135
bestow two pence to look after them.

SIR GILBERT.

How, a device at the wedding say'st thou!

PICKADILLE.

Why, have none of you heard of that yet?

SIR GILBERT.

'Tis the first news, i'faith, lad.

PICKADILLE.

Oh, there's a brave traveling scholar entertain'd into the 140
house o' purpose, one that has been all the world over,
and some part of Jerusalem; h'as his chamber, his diet,
and three candles allow'd him after supper.

WEATHERWISE.

By my faith, he need not complain for victuals then,
whate'er he be.   145

PICKADILLE.

He lies in one of the best chambers i'th' house, bravely
matted; and to warm his wits as much, a cup of sack and
an *aqua vitae* bottle stands just at his elbow.

WEATHERWISE.

He's shrewdly hurt, by my faith, if he catch an ague of
that fashion, I'll be hang'd.   150

PICKADILLE.

He'll come abroad anon.

SIR GILBERT.

Art sure on't?

131. believ'd] *Dyce;* bely'd *Q.*

---

136. *two pence*] the price of almanacs (Bosanquet, pp. 9–10).
148. *aqua vitae*] liquor, usually whisky or brandy (Copeman, p. 159).

PICKADILLE.

Why, he ne'er stays a quarter of an hour in the house together.

SIR GILBERT.

No? How can he study then?   155

PICKADILLE.

Pha, best of all, he talks as he goes, and writes as he runs; besides, you know 'tis death to a traveler to stand long in one place.

SIR GILBERT.

It may hit right, boys! —Honest Pickadille,
Thou wast wont to love me.   160

PICKADILLE.

I'd good cause, sir, then.

SIR GILBERT.

Thou shalt have the same still; take that. [*Gives him money.*]

PICKADILLE.

Will you believe me now; I ne'er lov'd you better in my life than I do at this present.

SIR GILBERT.

Tell me now truly; who are the presenters?   165
What parsons are employed in the device?

PICKADILLE.

Parsons! not any, sir; my mistress will not be at the charge; she keeps none but an old Welsh vicar.

SIR GILBERT.

Prithee, I mean, who be the speakers?

PICKADILLE.

Troth, I know none, but those that open their mouths. 170
Here he comes now himself; you may ask him.

Enter Master Beveril.

WEATHERWISE.

Is this he? By my faith, one may pick a gentleman out of his calves, and a scholar out on's cheeks; one may see by his looks what's in him. I warrant you there has ne'er a new almanac come out these dozen years, but he has 175
studied it over and over.

---

166. *parsons*] archaic form of "persons."

SIR GILBERT.

    Do not reveal us now.

PICKADILLE.

    Because you shall be sure on't, you have given me a nine-
pence here, and I'll give you the slip for't.   *Exit.*

SIR GILBERT.

    Well said; now the fool's pleas'd, we may be bold.   180

MASTER BEVERIL [*aside*].

    Love is as great an enemy to wit
As ignorance to art; I find my powers
So much employ'd in business of my heart
That all the time's too little to dispatch
Affairs within me. Fortune, too remiss,   185
I suffer for thy slowness; had I come
Before a vow had chain'd their souls together,
There might have been some hope, though ne'er so little;
Now there's no spark at all, nor e'er can be,
But dreadful ones struck from adultery;   190
And if my lust were smothered with her will,
Oh, who could wrong a gentleman so kind,
A stranger made up with a brother's mind?

SIR GILBERT.

    Peace, peace, enough, let me alone to manage it.—
A quick invention, and a happy one,   195
Reward your study, sir.

MASTER BEVERIL.   Gentlemen, I thank you.

SIR GILBERT.

    We understand your wits are in employment, sir,
In honor of this wedding.

MASTER BEVERIL.   Sir, the gentleman
To whom that worthy lady is betroth'd
Vouchsafes t'accept the power of my good will in't.   200

SIR GILBERT.

    I pray resolve us then, sir,
For we're friends that love and honor her,
Whether your number be yet full, or no,
Of those which you make choice of for presenters.

201-2.] *this edn.; in* O *lines end*
friends/ her.

MASTER BEVERIL.

  First, 'tis so brief, because the time is so,   205
  We shall not trouble many; and for those
  We shall employ, the house will yield in servants.

SIR GILBERT.

  Nay, then, under your leave and favor, sir,
  Since all your pains will be so weakly grac'd,
  And wanting due performance lose their luster, 210
  Here are four of us gentlemen, her friends,
  Both lovers of her honor and your art,
  That would be glad so to express ourselves,
  And think our service well and worthily plac'd.

MASTER BEVERIL.

  My thanks do me no grace for this large kindness; 215
  You make my labors proud of such presenters.

SIR GILBERT.

  She shall not think, sir, she's so ill belov'd,
  But friends can quickly make that number perfect.

MASTER BEVERIL.

  She's bound t'acknowledge it.

SIR GILBERT.   Only thus much, sir,
  Which will amaze her most, I'd have't so carried, 220
  As you can do't, that neither she, nor none,
  Should know what friends we were till all were done.

WEATHERWISE.

  Ay, that would make the sport.

MASTER BEVERIL.   I like it well, sir.
  My hand and faith amongst you gentlemen;
  It shall be so disposed of.

SIR GILBERT.   We are the men then. 225

MASTER BEVERIL.

  Then look you, gentlemen, the device is single,
  Naked, and plain, because the time's so short,
  And gives no freedom to a wealthier sport;
  'Tis only, gentlemen, the four elements
  In liveliest forms, earth, water, air, and fire. 230

WEATHERWISE.

  Mass, and here's four of us, too.

MASTER BEVERIL.   It fits well, sir.
  This the effect: that whereas all those four

Maintain a natural opposition
And untruc'd war, the one against the other,
To shame their ancient envies, they should see   235
How well in two breasts all these do agree.

WEATHERWISE.

That's in the bride and bridegroom; I am quick, sir.

SIR GILBERT.

In faith, it's pretty, sir; I approve it well.

MASTER BEVERIL.

But see how soon my happiness and your kindness
Is cross'd together.

SIR GILBERT.   Cross'd? I hope not so, sir.   240

MASTER BEVERIL.

I can employ but two of you.

MASTER PEPPERTON.   How comes that, sir?

MASTER BEVERIL.

Air and the fire should be by men presented,
But the two other in the forms of women.

WEATHERWISE [aside].

Nay, then we're gone again; I think these women
Were made to vex and trouble us in all shapes.   245

SIR GILBERT.

Faith, sir, you stand too nicely.

WEATHERWISE.   So think I, sir.

MASTER BEVERIL.

Yet when we tax ourselves, it may the better
Set off our errors, when the fine eyes judge 'em;
But water certainly should be a woman.

WEATHERWISE.

By my faith, then he is gelded since I saw him last; he 250
was thought to be a man once, when he got his wife with
child before he was married.

MASTER BEVERIL.

Fie, you are fishing in another stream, sir.

242. men] *Dyce;* me *O.*

---

246. *nicely*] precisely.
250–52.] Weatherwise is punning on the name "Walter" which was
pronounced "Water."

WEATHERWISE.

But now I come to yours, and you go to that, sir; I see
no reason then but fire and water should change shapes 255
and genders.

MASTER BEVERIL.

How prove you that, sir?

WEATHERWISE.

Why, there's no reason but water should be a man,
because fire is commonly known to be a quean.

MASTER BEVERIL.

So, sir, you argue well.   260

WEATHERWISE.

Nay more, sir; water will break in at a little crevice, so
will a man if he be not kept out; water will undermine,
so will an informer; water will ebb and flow, so will a
gentleman; water will search any place, and so will a
constable, as lately he did at my Seven Stars for a young 265
wench that was stole; water will quench fire, and so will
Wat the barber; *ergo*, let water wear a codpiece-point.

MASTER BEVERIL.

Faith, gentlemen, I like your company well.

WEATHERWISE.

Let's see who'll dispute with me at the full o'th' moon.

MASTER BEVERIL.

No, sir; and you be vainglorious of your talent, I'll put 270
you to't once more.

WEATHERWISE.

I'm for you, sir, as long as the moon keeps in this quarter.

MASTER BEVERIL.

Well, how answer you this then? Earth and water are
both bearers, therefore they shoud be women.

WEATHERWISE.

Why, so are porters and peddlers, and yet they are known 275
to be men.

---

267. *Wat the barber*] *Wat* is a diminutive of Walter; barbers func-
tioned as doctors and administered to those suffering from the fires
of lechery.
267. *ergo*] therefore.

MASTER BEVERIL.

I'll give you over in time, sir; I shall repent the bestow-
ing on't else.

WEATHERWISE.

If I that have proceeded in five and twenty such books of
astronomy should not be able to put down a scholar now 280
in one thousand six hundred thirty and eight, the dominical letter being G, I stood for a goose.

SIR GILBERT.

Then this will satisfy you though that be a woman;
Oceanus, the sea, that's chief of waters,
He wears the form of a man, and so may you.   285

MASTER BEVERIL.

Now I hear reason, and I may consent.

SIR GILBERT.

And so, though earth challenge a feminine face,
The matter of which earth consists, that's dust,
The general soul of earth is of both kinds.

MASTER BEVERIL.

Fit yourselves, gentlemen, I've enough for me.   290
Earth, water, air, and fire, part 'em amongst you.

WEATHERWISE.

Let me play air; I was my father's eldest son.

MASTER BEVERIL.

Ay, but this air never possess'd the lands.

WEATHERWISE.

I'm but dispos'd to jest with you, sir; 'tis the same my
almanac speaks on, is't not?   295

MASTER BEVERIL.

That 'tis, sir.

292. air] *Dyce;* fair *Q.*

---

281. *one thousand . . . eight*] an addition by James Shirley when he
revised the play for a Dublin performance, probably in that year.
281–82. *dominical . . . G*] As a liturgical device, Sundays were given
dominical letters. The first seven days of January were each assigned
a letter, A through G, and the letter that fell on the first Sunday was
the dominical letter for the year.
292. *air*] pun on "heir."

WEATHERWISE.

    Then leave it to my discretion to fit both the part and
    the person.

MASTER BEVERIL.

    You shall have your desire, sir.

SIR GILBERT.   We'll agree

    Without your trouble now, sir; we're not factious,   300
    Or envy one another for best parts,
    Like quarrelling actors that have passionate fits;
    We submit always to the writer's wits.

MASTER BEVERIL.

    He that commends you, may do't liberally,
    For you deserve as much as praise can show.   305

SIR GILBERT.

    We'll send to you privately.

MASTER BEVERIL.   I'll dispatch you.

SIR GILBERT [*aside*].

    We'll poison your device.   *Exit.*

MASTER PEPPERTON [*aside*].   She must have pleasures,

    Shows, and conceits, and we disgraceful doom.   [*Exit.*]

WEATHERWISE [*aside*].

    We'll make your elements come limping home.

                      Exeunt [Suitors].

MASTER BEVERIL.

    How happy am I in this unlook'd-for grace,   310
    This voluntary kindness from these gentlemen!

Enter Mistress Low-water *and her man-husband* [Master Low-
water, *both disguised*].

    'Twill set off all my labors far more pleasing
    Before the widow, whom my heart calls mistress,
    But my tongue dares not second it.

MASTER LOW-WATER [*aside to* Mistress Low-water].

    How say you now, Kate?   315

MISTRESS LOW-WATER.

    I like this music well, sir.

MASTER BEVERIL.   Oh, unfortunate!

    Yet though a tree be guarded from my touch,
    There's none can hinder me to love the fruit.

311.1–2.] *before l. 315 in* O.

MISTRESS LOW-WATER [*aside to* Master Low-water].
 Nay, now we know your mind, brother, we'll provide for
  you.   [*Exeunt the* Low-waters.]

MASTER BEVERIL.
 Oh, were it but as free as late times knew it,   320
 I would deserve, if all life's wealth could do it.   *Exit.*

[IV.i]
Enter at Sir Oliver's *house, himself, old* Sunset, *his redeemed lady*
[Lady Twilight], Master Sandfield, *the* Dutch Merchant, Philip,
Sir Oliver's *son, and* Savorwit, *aloof off, and Servants.*

SIR OLIVER.
 Oh my reviving joy! Thy quick'ning presence
 Makes the sad night of threescore and ten years
 Sit like a youthful spring upon my blood.
 I cannot make thy welcome rich enough
 With all the wealth of words.

LADY TWILIGHT.   It is express'd, sir,   5
 With more than can be equall'd; the ill store
 Lies only on my side, my thanks are poor.

SIR OLIVER.
 Bless'd be the goodness of his mind forever
 That did redeem thy life; may it return
 Upon his fortunes double! That worthy gentleman,   10
 Kind Master Beveril, shower upon him, heaven,
 Some unexpected happiness to requite him
 For that my joy unlook'd for! Oh, more kind
 And juster far is a mere stranger's goodness
 Than the sophistic faith of natural sons!   15
 Here's one could juggle with me, take up the ransom,
 He and his loose companion.

SAVORWIT [*aside*].   Say you me so, sir?
 I'll eat hard eggs for that trick.

---

319. S.D.] *this edn.; Exit O.*   13. joy] *Dyce;* joys *O.*

[IV.i]
 15. *sophistic*] false, speciously reasoned.

SIR OLIVER.   Spend the money,
And bring me home false news, and empty pockets.
In that young gallant's tongue there you were dead   20
Ten weeks before this day, had not this merchant
Brought first the truth in words, yourself in substance.

LADY TWILIGHT.
Pray let me stay you here, ere you proceed, sir.
Did he report me dead say you?

SIR OLIVER.   Else you live not.

LADY TWILIGHT.
See now, sir, you may lay your blame too rashly,   25
When nobody look'd after it; let me tell you, sir,
A father's anger should take great advice,
Ere it condemn flesh of so dear a price.
He's no way guilty yet, for that report
The general tongue of all the country spread,   30
For being remov'd 'far off, I was thought dead.

PHILIP.
Can my faith now be taken into favor, sir?
Is't worthy to be trusted?

SAVORWIT [aside].   No, by my troth, is't not;
'Twould make shift to spend another ransom yet.

SIR OLIVER.
Well sir, I must confess y'ave here dealt well with me;   35
And what is good in you, I love again.

SAVORWIT [aside].
Now am I half ways in, just to the girdle,
But the worst part's behind.

SIR OLIVER.   Marry, I fear me, sir,
This weather is too glorious to hold long.

LADY TWILIGHT.
I see no cloud to interpose it, sir,   40
If you place confidence in what I have told you.

SIR OLIVER.
Nay, 'tis clear sky on that side; would 'twere so
All over his obedience. I see that,
And so does this good gentleman.

33–34. No . . . yet] *Dyce; in O*
lines end shift/ yet.

LADY TWILIGHT. Do you, sir?
SIR OLIVER.
    That makes his honesty doubtful.
LADY TWILIGHT. I pray, speak, sir. 45
    The truth of your last kindness makes me bold with you.
DUTCH MERCHANT.
    The knight, your husband, madam, can best speak;
    He truliest can show griefs whose heart they break.
LADY TWILIGHT.
    I'm sorry yet for more; pray let me know't, sir,
    That I may help to chide him, though 'twould grieve me. 50
SIR OLIVER.
    Why then prepare for't. You came over now
    In the best time to do't you could pick out;
    Not only spent my money, but to blind me,
    He and his wicked instrument—
SAVORWIT [aside]. Now he fiddles me!
SIR OLIVER.
    Brings home a minion here, by great chance known; 55
    Told me she was his sister; she proves none.
LADY TWILIGHT.
    This was unkindly done, sir. Now I'm sorry
    My good opinion lost itself upon you;
    You are not the same son I left behind me;
    More grace took him. Oh, let me end in time, 60
    For fear I should forget myself and chide him!
    Where is she, sir? Though he beguil'd your eyes,
    He cannot deceive mine; we're now too hard for him.
    For since our first unfortunate separation,
    I've often seen the girl—[aside] would that were true— 65
    By many a happy accident, many a one;
    But never durst acknowledge her for mine own,
    And therein stood my joys distress'd again.
SIR OLIVER.
    You rehearse miseries, wife. —Call the maid down.

62. she] *Dyce;* he *Q.*

---

55. *minion*] mistress, loose woman.

SAVORWIT [*aside*].

    She's been too often down to be now called so;   70

    She'll lie down shortly, and call somebody up.

LADY TWILIGHT.

    He's now to deal with one, sir, that knows truth;

    He must be sham'd or quit; there's no mean saves him.

SIR OLIVER.

    I hear her come.

LADY TWILIGHT [*to* Philip].   You see how hard 'tis now

    To redeem good opinion being once gone;   75

    Be careful then, and keep it when 'tis won.

    Now see me take a poison with great joy,

    Which but for thy sake, I should swoon to touch.

Enter Grace.

GRACE [*aside*].

    What new affliction? Am I set to sale

    For any one that bids most shame for me?   80

SIR OLIVER.

    Look you! Do you see what stuff they've brought me

        home here?

LADY TWILIGHT.

    Oh, bless her, eternal powers! My life, my comforts,

    My nine-years' grief, but everlasting joy now!

    Thrice welcome to my heart; 'tis she indeed.

                                    [*Embracing* Grace.]

SIR OLIVER.

    What, is it?

PHILIP.   I'm unfit to carry a ransom!   85

SAVORWIT [*to* Grace].

    Down on your knees to save your belly harmless;

    Ask blessing, though you never mean to use it,

    But give't away presently to a beggar-wench. [Grace *kneels*.]

PHILIP.

    My faith is blemish'd; I'm no man of trust, sir.

LADY TWILIGHT.

    Rise with a mother's blessing.   [Grace *rises*.] 90

SAVORWIT [*aside*].

    All this while sh'as rise with a son's.

SIR OLIVER.

    But soft ye, soft ye, wife!
    I pray take heed you place your blessing right now.
    This honest Dutchman here told me he saw her
    At Antwerp in an inn.

LADY TWILIGHT.   True, she was so, sir.   95

DUTCH MERCHANT.

    Sir, 'tis my quality, what I speak once,
    I affirm ever; in that inn I saw her;
    That lets her not to be your daughter now.

SIR OLIVER.

    Oh, sir, is't come to that!

MASTER SUNSET.   Here's joys ne'er dream'd on!

SIR OLIVER.

    Oh, Master Sunset, I am at the rising   100
    Of my refulgent happiness! —Now, son Sandfield,
    Once more and ever!

SANDFIELD.   I am proud on't, sir.

SIR OLIVER.

    Pardon me, boy, I have wrong'd thy faith too much.

SAVORWIT [aside].

    Now may I leave my shell and peep my head forth.

SIR OLIVER.

    Where is this Savorwit, that honest whoreson,   105
    That I may take my curse from his knave's shoulders?

SAVORWIT.

    Oh, sir, I feel you at my very blade here;
    Your curse is ten stone weight, and a pound over.

SIR OLIVER.

    Come, thou'rt a witty varlet, and a trusty.

SAVORWIT.

    You shall still find me a poor faithful fellow, sir,   110
    If you have another ransom to send over,
    Or daughter to find out.

SIR OLIVER.   I'll do thee right, boy;
    I ne'er yet knew thee but speak honest English;
    Marry, in Dutch I found thee a knave lately.

---

98. *lets*] hinders.

SAVORWIT.

    That was to hold you but in play a little,   115
    Till farther truths came over, and I strong;
    You shall ne'er find me a knave in mine own tongue;
    I have more grace in me; I go out of England
    Still when I take such courses; that shows modesty, sir.

SIR OLIVER.

    Anything full of wit and void of harm   120
    I give thee pardon for, so was that now.

SAVORWIT.

    Faith, now I'm quit, I find myself the nimbler
    To serve you so again, and my will's good—
    [*Aside.*] Like one that lately shook off his old irons,
    And cuts a purse at bench, to deserve new ones.   125

SIR OLIVER.

    Since it holds all the way so fortunate still,
    And strikes so even with my first belief,
    This is the gentleman, wife, young Master Sandfield here,
    A man of worthy parts, beside his lands,
    Whom I make choice of for my daughter's bed.   130

SAVORWIT [*aside*].

    But he'll make choice there of another bedfellow.

LADY TWILIGHT.

    I wish 'em both the happiness of love, sir.

SIR OLIVER.

    'Twas spoke like a good lady! And your memory
    Can reach it, wife, but 'tis so long ago too,
    Old Master Sunset he had a young daughter   135
    When you unluckily left England so,
    And much about the age of our girl there,
    For both were nurs'd together.

LADY TWILIGHT.   'Tis so fresh
    In my remembrance, now y'have waken'd it,
    As if twelve years were but a twelve-hours' dream.   140

133–34.] *Dyce; in* O *lines end*
Lady—/ too.

---

125. *bench*] court of law.

SIR OLIVER.

    That girl is now a proper gentlewoman,
    As fine a body, wife, as e'er was measured
    With an indenture cut in farthing steaks.

MASTER SUNSET.

    Oh, say not so, Sir Oliver, you shall pardon me, sir.
    I'faith, sir, you are too blame.

SIR OLIVER.   Sings, dances, plays,   145
    Touches an instrument with a motherly grace.

MASTER SUNSET.

    'Tis your own daughter that you mean that by.

SAVORWIT [aside].

    There's open Dutch indeed, and he could take it!

SIR OLIVER.

    This wench, under your leave—

MASTER SUNSET.   You have my love in't.

SIR OLIVER.

    Is my son's wife that shall be.

SAVORWIT [aside].   Thus I'd hold with't;   150
    Is your son's wife that should be Master Sandfield's.

LADY TWILIGHT.

    I come in happy time to a feast of marriages.

SIR OLIVER.

    And now you put's i'th' mind, the hour draws on
    At the new-married widow's; there we're look'd for;
    There will be entertainments, sports, and banquets;   155
    There these young lovers shall clap hands together;
    The seed of one feast shall bring forth another.

MASTER SUNSET.

    Well said, Sir Oliver.

SIR OLIVER.   Y'are a stranger, sir,
    Your welcome will be best.

DUTCH MERCHANT.   Good sir, excuse me.

SIR OLIVER.

    You shall along, i'faith; you must not refuse me.   160

---

  141. *proper*] handsome.
  143. *indenture . . . steaks*] a servant's bond torn into pieces.
  148. *open Dutch*] unreserved frankness, punning on "motherly"
(l. 146).

[*Exeunt;*] *manent Mother* [Lady Twilight], *Sister* [Grace], Philip, *and* Savorwit.

PHILIP.

Oh, mother, these new joys that sets my soul up,
Which had no means, nor any hope of any,
Has brought me now so far in debt to you,
I know not which way to begin to thank you.
I am so lost in all, I cannot guess   165
Which of the two my service most constrains,
Your last kind goodness or your first dear pains.

LADY TWILIGHT.

Love is a mother's duty to a son,
As a son's duty is both love and fear.

SAVORWIT.

I owe you a poor life, madam, that's all;   170
Pray call for't when you please; it shall be ready for you.

LADY TWILIGHT.

Make much on't, sir, till then.

SAVORWIT [*aside*].   If butter'd sack will.

LADY TWILIGHT.

Methinks the more I look upon her son,
The more thy sister's face runs in my mind.

PHILIP.

Belike she's somewhat like her; it makes the better,
    madam.   175

LADY TWILIGHT.

Was Antwerp, say you, the first place you found her in?

PHILIP.

Yes, madam. Why do you ask?

LADY TWILIGHT.   Whose daughter were you?

GRACE.

I know not rightly whose, to speak truth, madam.

SAVORWIT [*aside*].

The mother of her was a good twigger the whilst.

LADY TWILIGHT.

No? With whom were you brought up then?

GRACE.   With those, madam, 180
To whom, I've often heard, the enemy sold me.

---

179. *twigger*] strumpet, literally a prolific ewe *(OED)*.

LADY TWILIGHT.

    What's that?

GRACE.

    Too often have I heard this piteous story
    Of a distressed mother I had once,
    Whose comfortable sight I lost at sea;   185
    But then the years of childhood took from me
    Both the remembrance of her, and the sorrows.

LADY TWILIGHT [aside].

    Oh, I begin to feel her in my blood!
    My heart leaps to be at her. —What was that mother?

GRACE.

    Some said an English lady, but I know not.   190

LADY TWILIGHT.

    What's thy name?

GRACE.   Grace.

LADY TWILIGHT.   May it be so in heaven,

    For thou art mine on earth! Welcome, dear child,
    Unto thy father's house, thy mother's arms,
    After thy foreign sorrows.   [Embracing Grace.]

SAVORWIT [aside].   'Twill prove gallant!

LADY TWILIGHT.

    What, son! Such earnest work; I bring thee joy now   195
    Will make the rest show nothing, 'tis so glorious.

PHILIP.

    Why, 'tis not possible, madam, that man's happiness
    Should take a greater height than mine aspires.

LADY TWILIGHT.

    No, now you shall confess it; this shall quit thee
    From all fears present, or hereafter doubts,   200
    About this business.

PHILIP.   Give me that, sweet mother.

LADY TWILIGHT.

    Here take her then, and set thine arms a-work;
    There needs no 'fection, 'tis indeed thy sister.

PHILIP.

    My sister!

SAVORWIT [aside].   Cuds me, I feel the razor!

---

203. 'fection] affection, pose.

LADY TWILIGHT.

    Why, how now, son? How comes a change so soon?   205

PHILIP.

    Oh, I beseech you, mother, wound me anywhere
    But where you pointed last. That's present death!
    Devise some other miserable torment,
    Though ne'er so pitiless, and I'll run and meet it.
    Some way more merciful let your goodness think on,   210
    May steal away my joys, but save my soul!
    I'll willingly restore back every one,
    Upon that mild condition; anything
    But what you spake last will be comfortable.

LADY TWILIGHT.

    Y'are troubled with strange fits in England here.   215
    Your first suit to me did entreat me hardly
    To say 'twas she, to have old wrath appeas'd,
    And now 'tis known your sister, y'are not pleas'd.
    How should I show myself?

PHILIP.   Say 'tis not she.

LADY TWILIGHT.

    Shall I deny my daughter?

PHILIP.   Oh, you kill me   220
    Beyond all tortures?

LADY TWILIGHT.   Why do you deal thus with me?

PHILIP.

    She is my wife; I married her at Antwerp;
    I have known the way unto her bed these three months.

SAVORWIT [aside].

    And that's too much by twelve weeks for a sister.

LADY TWILIGHT.

    I understand you now, too soon, too plain.   225

PHILIP.

    Oh, mother, if you love my peace forever,
    Examine her again, find me not guilty.

LADY TWILIGHT.

    'Tis now too late, her words make that too true.

PHILIP.

    Her words? Shall bare words overthrow a soul?

A body is not cast away so lightly.   230
How can you know 'tis she? Let sense decide it;
She then so young, and both so long divided.

LADY TWILIGHT.
She tells me the sad story.

PHILIP.   Does that throw me?
Many a distress may have the face of yours
That never was kin to you.

LADY TWILIGHT.   But, however, sir,   235
I trust you are not married.

PHILIP.   Here's the witness,
And all the wealth I had with her; this ring
That join'd our hearts together.   [Shows the ring.]

LADY TWILIGHT.   Oh, too clear now!
Thou'st brought in evidence to o'erthrow thyself;
Had no one word been spoke, only this shown,   240
'T had been enough to approv'd her for mine own.
See here, two letters that begun my name
Before I knew thy father; this I gave her,
And, as a jewel, fasten'd to her ear.

GRACE.
  Pardon me, mother, that you find it stray;   245
I kept it till I gave my heart away.

PHILIP.
Oh, to what mountain shall I take my flight,
To hide the monster of my sin from sight!

SAVORWIT [aside].
I'll to Wales presently; there's the best hills
To hide a poor knave in.   250

LADY TWILIGHT.
Oh, heap not desperation upon guilt!
Repent yet, and all's sav'd; 'twas but hard chance;
Amongst all sins, heaven pities ignorance;
She's still the first that has her pardon sign'd;
All sins else see their faults, she's only blind.   255
Go to thy chamber, pray, leave off, and win;
One hour's repentance cures a twelve-month's sin.

---

230. cast away] condemned to death; English law required more than
the testimony of one witness (bare words, l. 229).
254. She's] Ignorance.

GRACE.

    Oh, my distressed husband, my dear brother!

                    [Lady Twilight] *exit cum filia* [Grace].

PHILIP.

    Oh, Savorwit! Never came sorrow yet

    To mankind like it; I'm so far distress'd,   260

    I've no time left to give my heart attendance,

    Too little all to wait upon my soul!

    Before this tempest came, how well I stood,

    Full in the beams of blessedness and joy!

    The memory of man could never say   265

    So black a storm fell in so bright a day.

    I am that man that ev'n life surfeits of;

    Or if to live, unworthy to be seen

    By the savage eyesight; give's thy hand;

    Commend me to thy prayers.

SAVORWIT [*aside*].   Next time I say 'em.   270

PHILIP.

    Farewell, my honest breast, that cravest no more

    Than possible kindness; that I've found thee large in,

    And I must ask no more; there wit must stay,

    It cannot pass, where fate stops up the way.

    Joy thrive with thee; I'll never see thee more.   275

SAVORWIT.

    What's that, sir?

    Pray come back, and bring those words with you;

    You shall not carry 'em so out of my company.

    There's no last refuge, when your father knows it;

    There's no such need on't yet; stay but till then,   280

    And take one with you that will imitate you

    In all the desperate onsets man dare think on.

    Were it to challenge all the wolves in France

    To meet at one set battle, I'd be your half in't;

    All beasts of venom—what you had a mind to,   285

    Your part should be took still. For such a day

    Let's keep ourselves in heart, then am I for you.

    In the meantime, to beat off all suspicion,

    Let's to the bridehouse too; here's my petition.

258.1.] *after l. 257 in* O.

PHILIP.

    Thou hast a learning art when all hopes fly;   290
    Let one night waste, there's time enough left to die.

SAVORWIT.

    A minute's as good as a thousand year, sir,
    To pink a man's heart like a summer suit.   *Exeunt.*

[IV.ii]

Enter two or three Servants *placing things in order, with* Pickadille, *the clown, like an overseer.*

PICKADILLE.

    Bestir your bones nimbly, you ponderous beef-buttock'd
    knaves; what a number of lazy hinds do I keep company
    withal! Where's the flesh-color velvet cushion now for my
    lady's pease-porridge-tawny-satin bum? You attendants
    upon revels!   5

1 SERVANT.

    You can prate and domineer well, because you have a
    privileged place, but I'd fain see you set your hand to't.

PICKADILLE.

    Oh, base bone-pickers, I set my hand to't! When did you
    e'er see a gentleman set his hand to anything, unless it
    were to a sheepskin, and receive a hundred pound for his   10
    pains?

2 SERVANT.

    And afterward lie in the Counter for his pleasure.

PICKADILLE.

    Why, true, sir; 'tis for his pleasure indeed; for, spite of
    all their teeths, he may lie i'th' hole when he list.

1 SERVANT.

    Marry, and should for me.   15

IV.ii.] *Dyce; no scene division in*   7. privileged] *Dyce;* priviledge *O.*
O.

---

293. *pink*] pierce.

[IV.ii]

    10. *sheepskin*] loan papers.

    12. *Counter*] debtor's prison.

    14. *hole*] the worst place in the Counter, also a double entendre;
see *The Roaring Girl,* III.iii.106.

PICKADILLE.

Ay, thou wouldst make as good a bawd as the best jailor
of them all; I know that.

1 SERVANT.

How, fool?

PICKADILLE.

Hark! I must call you knave within; 'tis but staying somewhat the longer for't.   *Exeunt.*   20

[IV.iii]

Loud music. Enter the new-married widow [Lady Goldenfleece],
and Kate [Mistress Low-water], *her husband, both changed in
apparel,* [*but* Mistress Low-water *still in disguise,*] *arm in arm
together; after them* Sir Oliver Twilight, Master Sunset, *and the
Dutch Merchant; after them the mother* [Lady Twilight], Grace,
the daughter sad, with Jane Sunset; *after these, melancholy* Philip,
Savorwit, *and* Master Sandfield[, *and* Master Low-water, *disguised
as before*].

MISTRESS LOW-WATER.

This fair assembly is most freely welcome;

SIR OLIVER. ALL.

Thanks to you, good sir.

LADY GOLDENFLEECE [*to* Lady Twilight].

                    Come my long-wish'd-for madam,
You and this worthy stranger take best welcome;
Your freedom is a second feast to me.

MISTRESS LOW-WATER [*aside to* Master Low-water].

How is't with my brother?

MASTER LOW-WATER.   The fit holds him still;   5
Nay, love's more violent.

MISTRESS LOW-WATER.   'Las, poor gentleman!
I would he had my office without money;
If he should offer any, I'd refuse it.

IV.iii.] *this edn.; no scene division*   6–7. 'Las . . . money] *Dyce; in* O
in O.   *lines end* he/ money.

IV.iii.] Lack of continuity in characters or action requires the scene
division.

7. *office without money*] position at no charge.

MASTER LOW-WATER.

I have the letter ready;
He's worthy of a place that knows how to use it.   10

MISTRESS LOW-WATER.

That's well said.—
Come ladies; gentlemen; Sir Oliver; good;
Seat yourselves; shall we be found unreadiest?
What is yon gentleman with the funeral face there?
Methinks that look does ill become a bride-house.   15

SIR OLIVER.

Who does your worship mean, sir? My son Philip?
I am sure he had ne'er less reason to be sad.
Why are you sad, son Philip?

PHILIP.   How, sir, sad?

You shall not find it so, sir.

SAVORWIT [aside to Philip].   Take heed he do not then.

You must beware how you carry your face in this com-   20
pany; as far as I can see, that young bridegroom has
hawk's eyes; he'll go nigh to spell sister in your face; if
your nose were but crooked enough to serve for an S,
he'd find an eye presently, and then he has more light
for the rest.   25

PHILIP.

I'll learn then to dissemble.

SAVORWIT.

Nay, and you be to learn that now, you'll ne'er sit in a
branch'd-velvet gown as long as you live; you should have
took that at nurse, before your mother wean'd you; so
do all those that prove great children, and batten well.   30
Peace, here comes a scholar indeed; he has learn'd it, I
warrant you.

Enter Master Beveril with a pasteboard.

LADY GOLDENFLEECE.

Kind sir, you're welcome; you take all the pains, sir.

11–15.] this edn.; prose in O.

---

28. branch'd-velvet gown] embroidered judge's gown.
30. batten] to thrive or prosper.

MASTER BEVERIL.

    I wish they were but worthy of the grace

    Of your fair presence, and this choice assembly.   35

    Here is an abstract, madam, of what's shown,

    Which I commend to your favor.

LADY GOLDENFLEECE.   Thank you for't, sir.

MASTER BEVERIL [aside].

    I would I durst present my love as boldly.

MISTRESS LOW-WATER [aside].

    My honest brother!

LADY GOLDENFLEECE.   Look thee here, sweetheart.

MISTRESS LOW-WATER.

    What's there, sweet madam?

MASTER BEVERIL.   Music, and we're ready.   40

*Loud music a while. A thing like a globe opens of one side o'th'
stage and flashes out Fire, then* Sir Gilbert, *that presents the part,
issues forth with yellow hair and beard, intermingled with streaks
like wild flames, a three-forked fire in's hand; and, at the same
time, Air* [Weatherwise] *comes down hanging by a cloud, with a
coat made like an almanac, all the twelve moons set in it, and the
four quarters: winter, spring, summer, and autumn, with change
of weathers: rain, lightning, and tempest, etc. And from under
the stage, at both ends, arises Water* [Master Overdon] *and Earth*
[Master Pepperton], *two persons; Water with green flags upon
his head standing up instead of hair, and a beard of the same,
with a chain of pearl. Earth with a number of little things like
trees, like a thick grove, upon his head, and a wedge of gold in
his hand, his garment of a clay color.*

    The Fire speaking first; the scholar [Master Beveril] *stands
behind, gives him the first word, which he now follows.*

MASTER BEVERIL [whispering].

    "The flame of zeal—"

SIR GILBERT [as Fire].   "The wicked fire of lust,

    Does now spread heat through water, air, and dust."

40.3. streaks] *Dyce;* stroaks *O.*

---

36. *abstract*] a plot synopsis.

MASTER BEVERIL [*aside*].

How! He's out in the beginning! —"The wheel of time—"

WEATHERWISE [*aside*].

The devil set fire o'th' distaff.

SIR GILBERT.

"I that was wont in elder times to pass   45
For a bright angel, so they call'd me then,
Now so corrupted with the upstart fires
Of avarice, luxury, and inconstant heats,
Struck from the bloods of cunning clap-fall'n daughters,
Night-walking wives, but, most, libidinous widows,   50
That I, that purify ev'n gold itself,
Have the contemptible dross thrown in my face,
And my bright name walk common in disgrace.
How am I us'd o'late, that I am so handled,
Thrust into alleys, hospitals, and tubs!   55
I was once a name of comfort, warm'd great houses
When charity was landlord; I have given welcome
To forty russet yeomen at a time,
In a fair Christmas-hall. How am I chang'd!
The chimneys are swept up, the hearth as cold   60
As the forefathers' charity in the son.
All the good hospitable heat now turns
To my young landlord's lust, and there it burns.
Rich widows, that were wont to choose by gravity
Their second husbands, not by tricks of blood,   65
Are now so taken with loose Aretine flames
Of nimble wantonness and high-fed pride,
They marry now but the third part of husbands,
Boys, smooth-fac'd catamites, to fulfill their bed,
As if a woman should a woman wed.   70

61. son] *Dyce;* Sun *O.*

---

43. *out*] forgotten his lines.
46. *bright angel*] Psalm 104:4.
49. *clap-fall'n*] infected with gonorrhea.
55. *tubs*] Sweating tubs were used for treatment of syphilis.
58. *russet*] reddish, homespun, woolen cloth.
66. *Aretine*] Pietro Aretino (1492–1556) was the author of satires and poems of a scandalous or licentious nature.
69. *catamites*] corruption of Ganymedes, Jupiter's boy.

These are the fires o'late, my brightness darks,
And fills the world so full of beggarly sparks."
MASTER BEVERIL [aside].
Heart! How am I disgrac'd? What rogue should this be?
LADY GOLDENFLEECE.
By my faith, Monsieur Fire, y'are a hot whoreson!
MISTRESS LOW-WATER [aside].
I fear my brother is beside his wits,   75
He would not be so senseless to rail thus else.
WEATHERWISE (as Air).
"After this heat, you madams fat and fair,
Open your casements wide, and take in air;
But not that air false women make up oaths with,
No, nor that air gallants perfume their clothes with;   80
I am that air that keeps about the clouds;
None of my kindred was smelt out in crowds;
Not any of our house was ever tainted,
When many a thousand of our foes have fainted.
Yet some there are that be my chief polluters,   85
Widows that falsify their faith to suitors,
And will give fair words when the sign's in Cancer,
But, at the next remove, a scurvy answer;
Come to the poor men's houses, eat their banquet,
And at night with a boy toss'd in a blanket;   90
Nay, shall I come more near? Perhaps at noon,
For here I find a spot full in the moon.
I know youth's trick; what's she that can withstand it
When Mercury reigns, my lady's chamber planet?
He that believes a widow's words shall fail   95
When Venus' gown-skirts sweeps the Dragon's tail.

73. Heart] Dyce; Heat O.

---

72. *sparks*] gaily-dressed gallants.
87. *sign's in Cancer*] Venus in the house of Cancer results in women
who are "very fickle . . . ever mutable and inconstant" (Lilly, *Introduction*, p. 309).
92. *spot . . . moon*] When the moon is in Cancer, women tend to
be prolific.
94. *When Mercury reigns*] Mercury is the "author of subtilty, tricks,
devices, perjury, etc." (Lilly, *Christian Astrology*, p. 77).

Fair weather the first day she makes to any,
The second cloudy, and the third day rainy;
The fourth day a great storm, lightning and thunder;
A bolt strikes the suitor, a boy keeps her under."   100

MASTER BEVERIL [*aside*].
    Life: These are some counterfeit slaves crept in their
        rooms,
    A' purpose for disgrace; they shall all share with me.
    Heart! Who the devil should these be?   *Exit* Beveril.

LADY GOLDENFLEECE.   My faith, gentlemen,
    Air has perfum'd the room well.

SIR OLIVER.   So methinks, madam.

SAVORWIT [*aside*].
    A man may smell her meaning two rooms off,   105
    Though his nose wanted reparations,
    And the bridge left at Shoreditch as a pledge
    For *rosa solis*, in a bleaking-house.

MISTRESS LOW-WATER.
    Life! What should be his meaning in't?

MASTER LOW-WATER.   I wonder.

MASTER OVERDON (as *Water*).
    "Me thinks this room should yet retain such heat,   110
    Struck out from the first ardor, and so glow yet,
    You should desire my company, wish for water,
    That offers here to serve your several pipes,
    Without constraint of mill or death of water house.
    What if I sprinkled on the widow's cheeks   115
    A few cool drops to lay the guilty heat
    That flashes from her conscience to her face;
    Would't not refresh her shame? From such as she
    I first took weakness and inconstancy;
    I sometimes swell above my banks and spread;   120

106–8. *nose . . . house*] One manifestation of the tertiary stage of
syphilis is *gummata* or the breakdown of tissues and cartilages, resulting
in disfigurement.

107. *Shoreditch*] a parish in northeast London with the reputation
"as a haunt of loose women" (Sugden).

108. *rosa solis*] a cordial.

108. *bleaking-house*] a hospital for venereal disease sufferers.

They're commonly with child before they're wed;
In me the Sirens sing before they play,
In her more witchcraft, for her smiles betray;
Where I'm least seen, there my most danger lies,
So in those parts hid most from a man's eyes: 125
Her heart, her love, or what may be more close;
I know no mercy, she thinks that no loss;
In her, poor gallants; pirates thrive in me;
I help to cast away, and so does she."

LADY GOLDENFLEECE.

Nay, and you can hold nothing, sweet sir Water,   130
I'll wash my hands a' you, ever hereafter.

MASTER PEPPERTON (as Earth).

"Earth stands for a full point, me you should hire
To stop the gaps of water, air, and fire;
I love muck well, but your first husband better.
Above his soul he lov'd it, as his end   135
Did fearfully witness it; at his last gasp
His spirit flam'd, as it forsook his breast,
And left the sparkles quarreling 'bout his lips;
Now of such metal the devil makes him whips.
He shall have gold enough to glut his soul;   140
And as for earth, I'll stop his crane's throat full;
The wealth he left behind him, most men know,
He wrung inconscionably from the rights
Of poor men's livings; he drunk dry their brows.
That liquor has a curse, yet nothing sweeter;   145
When your posterity drinks, then 'twill taste bitter."

SIR GILBERT.

"And now to vex, 'gainst nature, form, rule, place,
See once four warring elements all embrace." [*They embrace.*]

Enter four [persons including Beveril] *at several corners, address'd
like the four winds, with wings, etc., and dance all to the drum
and fife; the four Elements seem to give back and stand in amaze;
the South Wind has a great red face, the North Wind a*   pale

148. warring] *Dyce;* waiting *O.*

---

130. *sweet sir Water*] For the pun, see III.i.250–52, n.
132. *full point*] a full stop, a final period.

bleak one, the Western Wind one cheek red and another white,
and so the Eastern Wind. At the end of the dance, the Winds
shove off the disguises of the other four [the Elements], which
seem to yield and almost fall off of themselves at the coming of
the Winds; so all the four old suitors are discovered. Exeunt all
the Winds but one, which is the scholar [Master Beveril] in that
disguise; so shows all.

LADY GOLDENFLEECE.

How! Sir Gilbert Lambston! Master Overdon!

All our old suitors! You have took pains, my masters.   150

SIR GILBERT.

We made a vow we'd speak our minds to you.

WEATHERWISE.

And I think we're as good as our words, though it cost
some of our purses; I owe money for the clouds yet, I
care not who knows it; the planets are sufficient enough
to pay the painter, and I were dead.   155

LADY GOLDENFLEECE.

Who are you, sir?

MASTER BEVERIL [*removing his disguise*].

Your most unworthy servant.

LADY GOLDENFLEECE.

Pardon me, is't you, sir?

MASTER BEVERIL.

My disgrace urg'd my wit to take some form
Wherein I might both best and properliest   160
Discover my abusers, and your own,
And show you some content, before y'had none.

LADY GOLDENFLEECE.

Sir, I owe much both to your care and love,
And you shall find your full requital worthy.—
Was this the plot now your poor envy works out?   165
I do revenge myself with pitying on you.—
Take Fire into the buttery, he has most need on't;
Give Water some small beer, too good for him;

---

167. *buttery*] liquor storeroom. The genial punishments meted out
by the widow are appropriate to each element.
168. *small beer*] weak, watery beer.

Air, you may walk abroad like a fortune teller;
But take down Earth and make him drink i'th' cellar.   170

[*Exeunt Suitors.*]

MISTRESS LOW-WATER.

The best revenge that could be.

LADY TWILIGHT.   I commend you, madam.

SIR OLIVER.

I thought they were some such sneakers.

SAVORWIT.

The four suitors! And here was a mess of mad elements!

MISTRESS LOW-WATER.

Lights, more lights there! Where be these blue-coats?

[*Enter servants with lights.*]

LADY GOLDENFLEECE.

You know your lodgings, gentlemen, tonight.   175

SIR OLIVER.

'Tis bounty makes bold guests, madam.

LADY GOLDENFLEECE [*to* Lady Twilight].   Good rest, lady.

SIR OLIVER.

A most contentful night begin a health, madam,
To your long joys, and may the years go round with't.

LADY GOLDENFLEECE.

As many thanks as you have wish'd 'em hours, sir,
Take to your lodging with you.

MISTRESS LOW-WATER.   A general rest to all.   180

Exeunt [*all but* Philip *and* Savorwit].

PHILIP.

I'm excepted.

SAVORWIT.

Take in another to you then; there's room enough
In that exception, faith, to serve us both.
The dial of my sleep goes by your eyes.   [*Exeunt.*]

184. S.D.] *this edn.; Exit. Manent
Widow and Mrs.* Low-water *O.*

---

169. *fortune teller*] Weatherwise's costume is designed like that tra-
ditionally worn by astrologers and fortune tellers.
173. *mess*] a group of four.
174. *blue-coats*] the dress of servants.

[V.i]

Widow [Lady Goldenfleece] *and* Mistress Low-water [*are discovered*].

LADY GOLDENFLEECE.

    Now, like a greedy usurer alone,

    I sum up all the wealth this day has brought me,

    And thus I hug it.   [*Embracing her.*]

MISTRESS LOW-WATER.   Prithee!

LADY GOLDENFLEECE.   Thus, I kiss it.   [*Kissing her.*]

MISTRESS LOW-WATER.

    I can't abide these kissings.

LADY GOLDENFLEECE.   How, sir? Not!

    I'll try that sure, I'll kiss you out of that humor.   5

MISTRESS LOW-WATER.

    Push, by my troth, I cannot.

LADY GOLDENFLEECE.   What cannot you, sir?

MISTRESS LOW-WATER.

    Not toy, nor bill and imitate house pigeons;

    A married man must think of other matters.

LADY GOLDENFLEECE.

    How, other matters, sir? What other matters?

MISTRESS LOW-WATER.

    Why, are there no other matters that belong to't?   10

    Do you think y'have married only a cock-sparrow,

    And fit but for one business, like a fool?

    You shall not find it so.

LADY GOLDENFLEECE.   You can talk strangely, sir.

    Come, will you to bed?

MISTRESS LOW-WATER.   No, faith, will not I.

LADY GOLDENFLEECE.

    What, not to bed, sir?   15

MISTRESS LOW-WATER.

    And I do, hang me! Not to bed with you!

LADY GOLDENFLEECE.

    How, not to bed with me! Sir, with whom else?

MISTRESS LOW-WATER.

    Why, am not I enough to lie with myself?

LADY GOLDENFLEECE.

    Is that the end of marriage?

MISTRESS LOW-WATER.   No, by my faith,
    'Tis but the beginning, yet death is the end on't,   20
    Unless some trick come i'th' middle and dash all.
LADY GOLDENFLEECE.
    Were you so forward lately, and so youthful,
    That scarce my modest strength could save me from you,
    And are you now so cold?
MISTRESS LOW-WATER.   I've thought on't since.
    It was but a rude part in me, i'faith,   25
    To offer such bold tricks to any woman,
    And by degrees I shall well break myself from't;
    I feel myself well chasten'd since that time,
    And not the third part now so loosely minded.
    Oh, when one sees their follies, 'tis a comfort;   30
    My very thoughts take more staid years upon 'em.
    Oh, marriage is such a serious divine thing!
    It makes youth grave, and sweetly nips the spring.
LADY GOLDENFLEECE.
    If I had chose a gentleman for care
    And worldly business, I had ne'er took you;   35
    I had the offers of enough more fit
    For such employment; I chose you for love,
    Youth, and content of heart, and not for troubles;
    You are not ripe for them; after y'have spent
    Some twenty years in dalliance, youth's affairs,   40
    Then take a book in your hand, and sum up cares;
    As for wealth now, you know that's got to your hands.
MISTRESS LOW-WATER.
    But had I known 't had been so wrongfully got,
    As I heard since, you should have had free leave
    To have made choice of another master for't.   45
LADY GOLDENFLEECE.
    Why, can that trouble you?
MISTRESS LOW-WATER.   It may too soon; but go;
    My sleeps are sound; I love not to be started
    With an ill conscience at the fall of midnight,
    And have mine eyes torn ope with poor men's curses;

19–20. No . . . on't] *Dyce; in O*
lines end begin-/ on't.

I do not like the fate on't, 'tis still apt   50
To breed unrest, dissension, wild debate,
And I'm the worst at quarrels upon earth,
Unless a mighty injury should provoke me.
Get you to bed, go.

LADY GOLDENFLEECE.   Not without you, in troth, sir.

MISTRESS LOW-WATER.

If you could think how much you wrong yourself   55
In my opinion of you, you would leave me now
With all the speed you might; I like you worse
For this fond heat, and drink in more suspicion of you.
You high-fed widows are too cunning people
For a poor gentleman to come simply to.   60

LADY GOLDENFLEECE.

What's that, sir?

MISTRESS LOW-WATER.   You may make a youth on him.

'Tis at your courtesy, and that's ill trusted;
You could not want a friend, beside a suitor,
To sit in your husband's gown, and look over your
   writings.

LADY GOLDENFLEECE.

What's this?

MISTRESS LOW-WATER.   I say there is a time when women   65
Can do too much and understand too little.
Once more, to bed; I'd willingly be a father
To no more noses than I got myself;
And so good night to you.

LADY GOLDENFLEECE [aside].   Now I see the infection.
A yellow poison runs through the sweet spring   70
Of his fair youth already; 'tis distracted;
Jealous of that which thought yet never acted.—
Oh, dear sir! On my knees I swear to thee—   [Kneels.]

MISTRESS LOW-WATER.

I prithee, use them in thy private chamber
As a good lady should; spare 'em not there;   75
'Twill do thee good; faith, none 'twill do thee here.

---

61. *make a youth*] take advantage of his inexperience.
70. *yellow*] color of jealousy.

LADY GOLDENFLEECE [*rising and aside*].
    Have I yet married poverty, and miss'd love?
    What fortune has my heart? That's all I crav'd,
    And that lies now a-dying; it has took
    A speeding poison, and I'm ignorant how;   80
    I never knew what beggary was till now.
    My wealth yields me no comfort in this plight;
    Had want but brought me love, I'd happen'd right.
                      Exit Widow [Lady Goldenfleece].
MISTRESS LOW-WATER.
    So, this will serve now for a preparative
    To ope the pores of some dislike at first;   85
    The physic will pay't home.—

             Enter Master Low-water.

                      How dost thou, sir?
    How goes the work?
MASTER LOW-WATER.   Your brother has the letter.
MISTRESS LOW-WATER.
    I find no stop in't then; it moves well hitherto;
    Did you convey it closely?
MASTER LOW-WATER.   He ne'er set eye of me.

    [*Enter* Master Beveril,] *above*[*, with a letter*].

MASTER BEVERIL.
    I cannot read too often.
MISTRESS LOW-WATER [*to* Master Low-water].
                  Peace, to your office.   90
MASTER BEVERIL.
    What blessed fate took pity of my heart,
    But with her presence to relieve me thus!
    All the large volumes that my time hath master'd
    Are not so precious to adorn my spirit

77. miss'd] *Dyce;* must *O.*   86. S.D.] *in l. 87 in O.*
85. pores] *suggested by Dyce;* pow-
ers *O.*

---

   80. *speeding*] quick, deadly.
   85. *pores*] Dyce's emendation seems necessary because of the medical
figure of speech.

As these few lines are to enrich my mind.   95
I thirst again to drink of the same fountain.
[*Reads*] "Kind Sir, I found your care and love so much
in the performance of a little, wherein your wit and art
had late employment, that I dare now trust your bosom
with business of more weight and eminence. Little 100
thought the world that since the wedding dinner, all my
mirth was but dissembled, and seeming joys but counterfeit. The truth to you, sir, is, I find so little signs of content in the bargain I made i'th' morning that I began to
repent before evening prayer; and to show some fruits of 105
his willful neglect and wild disposition, more than the
day could bring forth to me, has now forsook my bed;
I know no cause for't."
MISTRESS LOW-WATER [*aside*].
But I'll be sworn I do.
MASTER BEVERIL [*reads*].
"Being thus distress'd, sir, I desire your comfortable pres- 110
ence and counsel, whom I know to be of worth and judgment, that a lady may safely impart her griefs to you, and
commit 'em to the virtues of commiseration and secrecy.
—Your unfortunate friend, The Widow-wife. —I have
took order for your private admittance with a trusty ser- 115
vant of mine own, whom I have plac'd at my chamber
door to attend your coming." —He shall not wait too long
and curse my slowness!
MASTER LOW-WATER [*aside*].
I would you'd come away then.
MASTER BEVERIL.
How much am I beguil'd in that young gentleman!   120
I would have sworn had been the perfect abstract
Of honesty and mildness; 'tis not so.
MISTRESS LOW-WATER [*aside*].
I pardon you, sweet brother; there's no hold
Of what you speak now; you're in Cupid's pound.

114–18. I . . . slowness] *prose by*
Dyce; in O *lines end* admittance/
I have/ coming,/ slowness.

MASTER BEVERIL.
> Bless'd be the secret hand that brought thee hither;   125
> But the dear hand that writ it, ten times bless'd. [*Exit above.*]

MASTER LOW-WATER.
> That's I still; has bless'd me now ten times at twice.
> Away; I hear him coming.

MISTRESS LOW-WATER.   Strike it sure now.   *Exit.*

MASTER LOW-WATER.
> I warrant thee, sweet Kate; choose your best—

Enter Master Beveril.

MASTER BEVERIL.
> Who's there?

MASTER LOW-WATER. Oh sir, is't you? Y'are welcome then;   130
> My lady still expects you, sir.

MASTER BEVERIL.   Who's with her?

MASTER LOW-WATER.
> Not any creature living, sir.

MASTER BEVERIL.   Drink that;   [*Giving money.*]
> I've made thee wait too long.

MASTER LOW-WATER.   It does not seem so now, sir.
> Sir, if a man tread warily as any
> Wise man will, how often may he come   135
> To a lady's chamber, and be welcome to her!

MASTER BEVERIL.
> Thou giv'st me learned counsel for a closet.

MASTER LOW-WATER.
> Make use on't, sir, and you shall find no loss in't.
>
>   [*Exit* Master Beveril.]
> So, you are surely in, and you must under.

Enter Kate [Mistress Low-water] *with all the guests:* Sir Oliver,
Master Sunset, *Wife* [Lady Twilight], *Daughter* [Grace], Philip,
Sandfield, [*Jane, Dutch Merchant,*] *and* Savorwit.

MISTRESS LOW-WATER.
> Pardon my rude disturbance, my wrongs urge it;   140
> I did but try the plainness of her mind,

133–36. It . . . her] *this edn.; in*
0 lines end man/ will,/ her?

Suspecting she dealt cunningly with my youth,
And told her the first night, I would not know her;
But minding to return, I found the door
Warded suspiciously, and I heard a noise,   145
Such as fear makes, and guiltiness at th'approaching
Of an unlook'd-for husband

ALL.   This is strange, sir.

MISTRESS LOW-WATER.

Behold, it's barr'd; I must not be kept out!

SIR OLIVER.

There is no reason, sir.

MISTRESS LOW-WATER.   I'll be resolv'd in't.

If you be sons of honor, follow me!   150
Break open door; rush in.

SAVORWIT.

Then must I stay behind, for I think I was begot i'th'
woodyard, and that makes everything go so hard with me.

MISTRESS LOW-WATER *(within)*.

That's he; be sure on him.

Enter confusedly [Mistress Low-water] *with the widow* [Lady
Goldenfleece], *and her brother* [Master Beveril], *the scholar*[, *and
the rest*].

SIR OLIVER.   Be not so furious, sir.

MISTRESS LOW-WATER.

She whispered to him to slip into her closet.
What, have I taken you? Is not my dream true now?   155
Unmerciful adulteress, the first night!

SIR OLIVER.

Nay, good sir, patience!

MISTRESS LOW-WATER.   Give me the villain's heart,
That I may throw't into her bosom quick;
There let the lecher pant.

LADY TWILIGHT.   Nay, sweet sir!

MISTRESS LOW-WATER.

Pardon me; his life's too little for me.   160

153.S.D.] *Dyce; before l. 153 in O.*   160.] *this edn.;* Pardon me,/ His
. . . me. *O.*

158. *quick*] alive.

LADY GOLDENFLEECE.

How am I wrongfully sham'd? Speak your intent, sir,
Before this company; I pursue no pity.

MISTRESS LOW-WATER.

This is a fine thievish juggling, gentlemen!
She asks her mate that shares in guilt with her.
Too gross, too gross!

MASTER BEVERIL [aside].   Rash mischief!

MISTRESS LOW-WATER.   Treacherous sir,   165
Did I for this cast a friend's arm about thee,
Gave thee the welcome of a worthy spirit,
And lodg'd thee in my house, nay, entertain'd thee
More like a natural brother than a stranger,
And have I this reward? Perhaps the pride   170
Of thy good parts did lift thee to this impudence.
Let her make much on 'em; she gets none of me.
Because thou'rt deeply read in most books else,
Thou wouldst be so in mine; there it stands for thee;

[Pointing to Lady Goldenfleece.]

Turn o'er the leaves, and where you left, go forward;   175
To me, it shall be like the book of fate,
Ever clasp'd up.

SIR OLIVER.   Oh, dear sir, say not so.

MISTRESS LOW-WATER.

Nay, I'll swear more; forever I refuse her;
I'll never set a foot into her bed,
Never perform the duty of man to her,   180
So long as I have breath.

SIR OLIVER.

What an oath was there, sir! Call't again.

MISTRESS LOW-WATER.

I knew by amorous sparks struck from their eyes,
The fire would appear shortly in a blaze,
And now it flames indeed. —Out of my house,   185
And take your gentleman of good parts along with you;
That shall be all your substance; he can live
In any emperor's court in Christendom.

187–88.] Dyce; in O lines end
substance; / Christendom.

You know what you did, wench, when you chose him
To thrust out me; you have no politic love!   190
You are to learn to make your market, you!
You can choose wit, a burden light and free,
And leave the grosser element with me,
Wealth, foolish trash, I thank you. —Out of my doors!

SIR OLIVER.
    Nay, good sir, hear her.

LADY TWILIGHT. MASTER SUNSET.   Sweet sir!   195

MISTRESS LOW-WATER.
    Pray, to your chambers, gentlemen; I should be here
    Master of what is mine.

SIR OLIVER.   Hear her but speak, sir!

MISTRESS LOW-WATER.
    What can she speak but woman's common language?
    She's sorry and asham'd for't; that helps nothing.

LADY GOLDENFLEECE.
    Sir, since it is the hard hap of my life   200
    To receive injury where I plac'd my love—

MISTRESS LOW-WATER.
    Why, la, I told you what escapes she'd have.

SIR OLIVER.
    Nay, pray, sir, hear her forward.

LADY GOLDENFLEECE.   Let our parting
    Be full as charitable as our meeting was,
    That the pale envious world, glad of the food   205
    Of others' miseries, civil dissensions,
    And nuptial strifes, may not feed fat with ours;
    But since you are resolv'd so willfully
    To leave my bed, and ever to refuse me,
    As by your rage I find it your desire,   210
    Though all my actions deserve nothing less,
    Here are our friends, men both of worth and wisdom,
    Place so much power in them, to make an evenness
    Between my peace and yours. All my wealth within doors,

203-4.] Dyce; in O lines end forward./ was.

_____

190. politic] crafty, used ironically.
202. escapes] evasions.

In gold and jewels, lie in those two caskets   215
I lately led you to, the value of which
Amounts to some five thousand apiece;
Exchange a charitable hand with me,
And take one casket freely; fare thee well, sir.

SIR OLIVER.
How say you to that now?

MISTRESS LOW-WATER.   Troth, I thank her, sir!   220
Are not both mine already? You shall wrong me,
And then make satisfaction with mine own?
I cannot blame you, a good course for you.

LADY TWILIGHT.
I know 'twas not my luck to be so happy;
My miseries are no starters; when they come,   225
Stick longer by me.

SIR OLIVER.   Nay, but give me leave, sir;
The wealth comes all by her!

MISTRESS LOW-WATER.   So does the shame,
Yet that's most mine; why should not that be too?

SIR OLIVER.
Sweet sir, let us rule so much with you:
Since you intend an obstinate separation,   230
Both from her bed and board, give your consent
To some agreement reasonable and honest.

MISTRESS LOW-WATER.
Must I deal honestly with her lust?

LADY TWILIGHT.   Nay, good sir.

MISTRESS LOW-WATER.
Why, I tell you, all the wealth her husband left her
Is not of power to purchase the dear peace   235
My heart has lost in these adulterous seas;
Yet, let her works be base, mine shall be noble.

SIR OLIVER.
That's the best word of comfort I heard yet.

MISTRESS LOW-WATER.
Friends may do much. —Go, bring those caskets forth.—
                                        [*Exit servants.*]
I hate her sight; I'll leave her, though I lose by't.   240

---

225. *starters*] lacking in perseverance.

SIR OLIVER.
    Spoke like a noble gentleman, i'faith!
    I'll honor thee for this.
MASTER BEVERIL [aside].   Oh, cursed man!
    Must thy rash heat force this division?
MISTRESS LOW-WATER.
    You shall have free leave now, without all fear;
    You shall not need oil'd hinges, privy passages,   245
    Watchings, and whisperings; take him boldly to you.
LADY GOLDENFLEECE.
    Oh, that I had that freedom! Since my shame
    Puts by all other fortunes, and owns him
    A worthy gentleman. If this cloud were past him,
    I'd marry him, were't but to spite thee only,   250
    So much I hate thee now.

Enter servants with two caskets, and the suitors [Sir Gilbert
Lambston, Weatherwise, Master Pepperton, *and* Master Overdon].

SIR OLIVER.
    Here come the caskets, sir; hold your good mind now,
    And we shall make a virtuous end between you.
MISTRESS LOW-WATER.
    Though nothing less she merit but a curse,
    That might still hang upon her and consume her still,   255
    As 't has been many a better woman's fortune,
    That has deserv'd less vengeance and felt more,
    Yet my mind scorns to leave her shame so poor.
SIR OLIVER.
    Nobly spoke still.
SIR GILBERT.   This strikes me into music—ha, ha!
MASTER PEPPERTON.
    Parting of goods before the bodies join?   260
WEATHERWISE.
    This 'tis to marry beardless domineering boys! I knew
    'twould come to this pass. Well fare a just almanac yet,
    for now is Mercury going into the second house near

unto Ursa Major, that great hunks, the Bear at the
bridge-foot in heaven, which shows horrible bear baitings 265
in wedlock; and the sun near ent'ring into th' Dog, sets
'em all together by th'ears.

SIR OLIVER.

You see what's in't?   [*Opening the caskets.*]

MISTRESS LOW-WATER.   I think 'tis as I left it.

LADY GOLDENFLEECE.

Then do but gage your faith to this assembly
That you will ne'er return more to molest me,   270
But rest in all revenges full appeas'd
And amply satisfied with that half my wealth,
And take't as freely as life wishes health.

SIR OLIVER.

La, you, sir; come, come, faith, you shall swear that!

MISTRESS LOW-WATER.

Nay, gentlemen, for your sakes, now I'll deal fairly with
    her.   275

SIR OLIVER.

I would we might see that, sir.

MISTRESS LOW-WATER.   I could set her free,
But now I think on't, she deserves it not.

MASTER SUNSET.

Nay, do not check your goodness, pray, sir; on with't.

MISTRESS LOW-WATER.

I could release her ere I parted with her,
But 'twere a courtesy ill plac'd, and set her   280
At as free liberty to marry again,
As you all know she was before I knew her.

SIR OLIVER.

What, couldst thou, sir?

MISTRESS LOW-WATER.   But 'tis too good a blessing for her.

---

264. *Ursa Major*] the great bear, the big dipper.
264. *hunks*] " 'Harry Hunks' was the name of a bear at Paris Garden"
(Bullen).
264–65. *Bear . . . bridge-foot*] The Bear was a well-known tavern at
the Southwark end of London bridge (Sugden).
266. *Dog*] Sirius or the Dog-star has a pernicious influence.
269. *gage*] pledge.

Up with the casket, sirrah.

LADY GOLDENFLEECE.   Oh, sir, stay!

MISTRESS LOW-WATER.

I have nothing to say to you.

SIR OLIVER.   Do you hear, sir?   285

Pray, let's have one word more with you for our money.

LADY GOLDENFLEECE.

Since y'have expos'd me to all shame and sorrow,
And made me fit but for one hope and fortune,
Bearing my former comforts away with you,
Show me a parting charity but in this: 290
For all my losses, pay me with that freedom,
And I shall think this treasure as well given
As ever 'twas ill got.

MISTRESS LOW-WATER.   I might afford it you,
Because I never mean to be more troubled with you;
But how shall I be sure of the honest use on't,   295
How you'll employ that liberty? Perhaps sinfully,
In wantonness unlawful, and I answer for't;
So I may live a bawd to your loose works still
In giving 'em first vent! not I, shall pardon me;
I'll see you honestly join'd ere I release you;   300
I will not trust you for the last trick you play'd me;
Here's your old suitors!

MASTER PEPPERTON.   Now we thank you, sir.

WEATHERWISE.

My almanac warns me from all cuckoldy conjunctions.

LADY GOLDENFLEECE.

Be but commander of your word now, sir,
And before all these gentlemen, our friends,   305
I'll make a worthy choice.

MASTER SUNSET.   Fly not ye back now.

MISTRESS LOW-WATER.

I'll try thee once. I am married to another;
There's thy release!

SIR OLIVER.   Hoyda! There's a release with a witness!

Thou'rt free, sweet wench.

LADY GOLDENFLEECE.   Married to another!

Then in revenge to thee,   310

To vex thine eyes, 'cause thou hast mock'd my heart,
And with such treachery repaid my love,
This is the gentleman I embrace and choose.

[*Embracing* Master Beveril.]

MISTRESS LOW-WATER.

Oh, torment to my blood, mine enemy!
None else to make thy choice of but the man   315
From whence my shame took head?

LADY GOLDENFLEECE.   'Tis done to quit thee.
Thou that wrong'st woman's love, her hate can fit thee.

SIR OLIVER.

Brave wench, i'faith! Now thou hast an honest gentle-
man,
Rid of a swaggering knave, and there's an end on't.
A man of good parts, this t'other had nothing.   320
Life, married to another!

SIR GILBERT.   Oh, brave rascal with two wives!

WEATHERWISE.

Nay, and our women be such subtle animals, I'll lay wait
at the carrier's for a country chambermaid, and live still
a bachelor. When wives are like almanacs, we may have
every year a new one, then I'll bestow my money on 'em; 325
in the meantime, I'll give 'em over and ne'er trouble my
almanac about 'em.

SIR GILBERT.

I come in a good time to see you hang'd, sir,
And that's my comfort. Now, I'll tickle you, sir.

MISTRESS LOW-WATER.

You make me laugh indeed.

SIR GILBERT.   Sir, you remember   330
How cunningly you chok'd me at the banquet
With a fine bawdy letter?

MISTRESS LOW-WATER.   Your own fist, sir.

SIR GILBERT.

I'll read the statute book to you now for't.

---

323. *carrier's . . . chambermaid*] Weatherwise plans to meet the un-
wary country girls as they arrive in the big city.
332. *fist*] handwriting.

Turn to the act in *Anno Jac. primo*,
There lies a halter for your windpipe.

MISTRESS LOW-WATER.   Fie, no.   335

SIR OLIVER.

Faith, but you'll find it so, sir, an't be followed.

WEATHERWISE.

So says my almanac, and he's a true man.
Look you! [*Reads.*] "The thirteenth day, work for the
hangman."

MISTRESS LOW-WATER.

The fourteenth day, make haste; 'tis time you were there
then.

WEATHERWISE.

How, is the book so saucy to tell me so?   340

MASTER BEVERIL.

Sir, I must tell you now, but without gall,
The law would hang you, if married to another.

MISTRESS LOW-WATER.

You can but put me to my book, sweet brother,
And I've my neck-verse perfect, here and here.
         [*Removes her disguise, revealing her bosom.*]
Heaven give thee eternal joy, my dear sweet brother!   345
     [*Embraces* Beveril; Master Low-water *removes his disguise.*]

ALL.

Who's here?

SIR GILBERT [*aside*].   Oh, devil! Herself! Did she betray me?
A pox of shame, nine coaches shall not stay me!
                          Exit Sir Gilbert.

MASTER BEVERIL.

I've two such deep healths in two joys to pledge,
Heaven keep me from a surfeit.

---

334. *Anno Jac. primo*] in the first year of James (*Jacobi*) I, 1603–1604;
an "'Acte to restrayne all persons from Marriage untill theire former
Wyves and former Husbandes be deade'" (Dyce).
344. *neck-verse*] By merely reciting Psalm 51:1; in Latin, a condemned man was entitled to the "benefit of clergy," which put him
outside civil law. Mistress Low-water's neck-verse, however, is her
breasts.

SIR OLIVER.   Mistress Low-water!

Is she the jealous cuckold all this coil's about?   350

And my right worshipful servingman, is it you, sir?

MASTER LOW-WATER.

A poor wrong'd gentleman, glad to serve for his own, sir.

SIR OLIVER.

By my faith, y'have serv'd the widow a fine trick between
   you.

MISTRESS LOW-WATER.

No more my enemy now, my brother's wife,

And my kind sister!

SIR OLIVER.   There's no starting now from't;   355

'Tis her own brother, did not you know that?

LADY GOLDENFLEECE.

'Twas never told me yet.

SIR OLIVER.   I thought you'd known't.

MISTRESS LOW-WATER.

What matter is't? 'Tis the same man was chose still,

No worse now than he was. I'm bound to love you;

Y'have exercis'd in this a double charity,   360

Which, to your praise, shall to all times be known,

Advanc'd my brother, and restor'd mine own.

Nay, somewhat for my wrongs, like a good sister,

For well you know the tedious suit did cost

Much pains and fees; I thank you, 'tis not lost;   365

You wish'd for love, and, faith, I have bestow'd you

Upon a gentleman that does dearly love you;

That recompense I've made you; and you must think,
   madam,

I lov'd you well, though I could never ease you,

When I fetch'd in my brother thus to please you.   370

SIR OLIVER.

Here's unity forever strangely wrought!

LADY GOLDENFLEECE.

I see too late there is a heavy judgment

Keeps company with extortion and foul deeds,

360. exercis'd] *Dyce;* examin'd *O.*

---

350. *coil*] tumult.

And like a wind which vengeance has in chase,
Drives back the wrongs into the injurer's face.   375
My punishment is gentle, and to show
My thankful mind for't, thus I'll revenge this,
With an embracement here, and here a kiss.
[*Embraces* Mistress Low-water; *kisses* Master Beveril.]

SIR OLIVER.

Why, now the bells they go trim, they go trim!—
[*To* Beveril.] I wish'd thee, sir, some unexpected blessing   380
For my wife's ransom, and 'tis fall'n upon thee.

WEATHERWISE.

A pox of this! My almanac ne'er gull'd me till this hour;
the thirteenth day, work for the hangman, and there's
nothing toward it; I'd been a fine ass, if I'd given twelve
pence for a horse to have rid to Tyburn tomorrow. But   385
now I see the error, 'tis false figured; it should be thirteen days and a half, work for the hangman, for he ne'er
works under thirteen pence half-penny; beside, Venus
being a spot in the sun's garment, shows there should be
a woman found in hose and doublet.   390

SIR OLIVER.

Nay, faith, sweet wife, we'll make no more hours on't
now, 'tis as fine a contracting time as ever came amongst
gentlefolks. —Son Philip, Master Sandfield, come to the
book here!

PHILIP [*aside to* Savorwit].

Now I'm waked into a thousand miseries and their tor-   395
ments.

SAVORWIT [*to* Philip].

And I come after you, sir, drawn with wild horses; there
will be a brave show on's anon, if this weather continue.

378.1.] Dyce's stage direction seems correct because the suspense rests
with the widow's possible rejection of Mistress Low-water and of Master
Beveril.

379. *trim*] ring properly.

382. *gull'd*] made a fool of.

388. *thirteen pence half-penny*] A thief could be hanged if he
stole more than that amount (*Tom Tell-Trothes New-yeares Gift*, New
Shakespeare Society, vol. 6, pt. 1, p. 43).

394. *book*] marriage contract.

SIR OLIVER.

    Come, wenches, where be these young gentlemen's hands
    now?   400

LADY TWILIGHT [aside].

    Poor gentleman, my son!—
    Some other time, sir.

SIR OLIVER.   I'll have't now, i'faith, wife.

    [Puts Philip's hand into Jane's and Sandfield's into Grace's.]

LADY GOLDENFLEECE.

    What are you making here?

SIR OLIVER.   I have sworn, sweet madam,
    My son shall marry Master Sunset's daughter,
    And Master Sandfield, mine.

LADY GOLDENFLEECE.   So you go well, sir;   405
    But what make you this way then?   [Points to Jane.]

SIR OLIVER.   This? for my son.

LADY GOLDENFLEECE.

    Oh, back, sir, back! This is no way for him.

MASTER SUNSET. SIR OLIVER.   How?

LADY GOLDENFLEECE.

    Oh, let me break an oath to save two souls,
    Lest I should wake another judgment greater!
    You come not here for him, sir.

SIR OLIVER.   What's the matter?   410

LADY GOLDENFLEECE.

    Either give me free leave to make this match,
    Or I'll forbid the banns.

SIR OLIVER.   Good, madam, take it.

LADY GOLDENFLEECE.

    Here, Master Sandfield, then—

SIR OLIVER.   Cuds bodkins!

LADY GOLDENFLEECE.

    Take you this maid.   [Gives Jane to Sandfield.]

SANDFIELD.   You could not please me better, madam.

399. gentlemen's] Dyce; Genmens   412. banns] this edn.; Banes O.
O.

---

413. Cuds bodkins] God's little body.

SIR OLIVER.

Hoyda! Is this your hot love to my daughter, sir?   415

LADY GOLDENFLEECE.

Come hither, Philip; here's a wife for you.

[*Gives* Grace *to* Philip.]

SIR OLIVER.

Zunes, he shall ne'er do that; marry his sister!

LADY GOLDENFLEECE.

Had he been rul'd by you, he had married her,
But now he marries Master Sunset's daughter,
And Master Sandfield, yours; I've sav'd your oath, sir.   420

PHILIP.

Oh, may this blessing hold!

SAVORWIT [*aside*].   Or else all the liquor runs out.

SIR OLIVER.

What riddle's this, madam?

LADY GOLDENFLEECE.

A riddle of some fourteen years of age now.
You can remember, madam, that your daughter
Was put to nurse to Master Sunset's wife.   425

LADY TWILIGHT.

True, that we talk'd on lately.

SIR OLIVER.   I grant that, madam.

LADY GOLDENFLEECE.

Then you shall grant what follows. At that time
You likewise know old Master Sunset here
Grew backward in the world, till his last fortunes
Rais'd him to this estate.

SIR OLIVER.   Still this we know too.   430

LADY GOLDENFLEECE.

His wife, then nurse both to her own and yours,
And both so young, of equal years, and daughters,
Fearing the extremity of her fortunes then
Should fall upon her infant, to prevent it,
She chang'd the children, kept your daughter with her,   435
And sent her own to you for better fortunes.
So long, enjoin'd by solemn oath unto't

---

417. *Zunes*] variation of "zounds," God's wounds.

Upon her death bed, I have conceal'd this;
But now so urg'd, here's yours, and this is his.

SAVORWIT.

Whoop, the joy is come of our side!   440

WEATHERWISE.

Hay, I'll cast mine almanac to the moon too, and strike
out a new one for next year.

PHILIP.

It wants expression, this miraculous blessing!

SAVORWIT.

Methinks I could spring up and knock my head
Against yon silver ceiling now for joy!   445

WEATHERWISE.

By my faith, but I do not mean to follow you there, so I
may dash out my brains against Charles' Wain, and come
down as wise as a carman.

SIR OLIVER.

I never wonder'd yet with greater pleasure.

LADY TWILIGHT.

What tears have I bestow'd on a lost daughter,   450
And left her behind me.

LADY GOLDENFLEECE.   This is Grace,
This Jane; now each has her right name and place.

MASTER SUNSET.

I never heard of this.

LADY GOLDENFLEECE.   I'll swear you did not, sir.

SIR OLIVER.

How well I have kept mine oath against my will!
Clap hands, and joy go with you. Well said, boys!   455

PHILIP [to Grace].

How art thou bless'd from shame and I from ruin.

SAVORWIT.

I, from the baker's ditch, if I'd seen you in.

440. Whoop] *Dyce;* Hoop *O.*   444–45.] *Dyce; prose in O.*

444–45.] very similar to Vendice's cry in *The Revenger's Tragedy,*
III.v.3–4, a play often ascribed to Middleton.
447. *Charles' Wain*] the big dipper. A *wain* is a cart.
457. *baker's ditch*] As a punishment, dishonest bakers were dunked
into water ditches (Brand, p. 642).

PHILIP.

Not possible the whole world to match again
Such grief, such joy, in minutes lost and won.

MASTER BEVERIL.

Whoever knew more happiness in less compass?   460
Ne'er was poor gentleman so bound to a sister
As I am, for the wittiness of thy mind;
Not only that thy due, but all our wealth
Shall lie as open as the sun to man
For thy employments; so the charity   465
Of this dear bosom bids me tell thee now.

MISTRESS LOW-WATER.

I am her servant for't.

LADY GOLDENFLEECE.   Hah, worthy sister!
The government of all, I bless thee with.

MASTER BEVERIL.

Come, gentlemen, on all perpetual friendship.
Heaven still relieves what misery would destroy;   470
Never was night yet of more general joy.   [Exeunt.]

EPILOGUE

WEATHERWISE.

Now let me see what weather shall we have now;
[Taking out almanac.]
Hold fair now, and I care not. —Mass, full moon, too,
Just between five and six this afternoon!
This happens right; [reads] "The sky for the best part
clear,
Save here and there a cloud or two dispers'd."   5

462. wittiness] suggested by Dyce;
weakness O.
Epilogue.]
1.S.P. WEATHERWISE] Dyce; not in
O.

462. wittiness] Both Dyce and Bullen felt some emendation was
necessary because Mistress Low-water does not suffer from "weakness"
of mind. Dyce suggested "wittiness," but did not emend; "wittiness"
fits the play title.

That's some dozen of panders and half a score
Pickpockets; you may know them by their whistle,
And they do well to use that while they may,
For Tyburn cracks the pipe and spoils the music.
What says the destiny of the hour this evening?   10
Hah, [*reads*] "Fear no colors!" By my troth, agreed then,
The red and white looks cheerfully; for know ye all,
The planet's Jupiter; you should be jovial;
There's nothing lets it but the sun i'th' Dog;
Some bark in corners that will fawn and cog,   15
Glad of my fragments for their ember week;
The sign's in Gemini too, both hands should meet;
There should be noise i'th' air, if all things hap,
Though I love thunder when you make the clap.
Some faults perhaps have slipp'd, I am to answer;   20
And if in anything your revenge appears,
Send me in with all your fists about mine ears.

FINIS

6–7.]*Dyce; in O lines end* Pick-
Pockets,/ whistle.

---

9. *pipe*] windpipe.
11. *Fear no colors*] a military proverb meaning "have no fear of hostile flags."
12. *red and white*] the audience, perhaps only its ladies; a conjunction of many-colored Jupiter with the white and red Gemini results in graceful, courteous, good-natured, and obliging people, just what Weatherwise wishes in the audience.
13. *jovial*] pun on Jove or Jupiter.
14. *sun i'th' Dog*] See note on V.i.266. Weatherwise refers to those critics who will *bark* at the play like *dogs*, but later creep back and *cog*, i.e., flatter or *fawn*.
16. *ember week*] a period of fasting.
17. *sign's in Gemini . . . hands*] The Gemini twins have dominion over the hands.
20. *answer*] "Here a line (ending with the word "Cancer") has dropt out" (Dyce).

Appendix

Chronology

Approximate years are indicated by *, occurrences in doubt by (?).

Political and Literary Events	Life and Major Works of Middleton

1558
Accession of Queen Elizabeth I.
Robert Greene born.
Thomas Kyd born.

1560
George Chapman born.

1561
Francis Bacon born.

1564
Shakespeare born.
Christopher Marlowe born.

1572
Thomas Dekker born.*
John Donne born.
Massacre of St. Bartholomew's
Day.

1573
Ben Jonson born.*

1574
Thomas Heywood born.*

1576
The Theatre, the first permanent
public theater in London, estab-
lished by James Burbage.
John Marston born.

1577
The Curtain theater opened.

Holinshed's *Chronicles of England, Scotland and Ireland.*
Drake begins circumnavigation of the earth; completed 1580.

1578
John Lyly's *Euphues: The Anatomy of Wit.*

1579
John Fletcher born.
Sir Thomas North's translation of Plutarch's *Lives.*

1580   Baptized, 18 April, at St. Lawrence Church in Old Jewry, London.

1583
Philip Massinger born.

1584
Francis Beaumont born.*

1586
Death of Sir Philip Sidney.
John Ford born.
Kyd's THE SPANISH TRAGEDY.

1587
The Rose theater opened by Henslowe.
Marlowe's *TAMBURLAINE,* Part I.*
Execution of Mary, Queen of Scots.
Drake raids Cadiz.

1588
Defeat of the Spanish Armada.
Marlowe's *TAMBURLAINE,* Part II.*

1589
Greene's FRIAR BACON AND FRIAR BUNGAY.*
Marlowe's THE JEW OF MALTA.*

1590
Spenser's *Faerie Queene* (Books I–III) published.

Sidney's *Arcadia* published.
Shakespeare's HENRY VI, Parts
I–III,* TITUS ANDRONICUS.*

1591
Shakespeare's RICHARD III.*

1592
Marlowe's DOCTOR FAUSTUS*
and EDWARD II.*
Shakespeare's TAMING OF THE
SHREW* and THE COMEDY OF
ERRORS.*
Death of Greene.

1593
Shakespeare's LOVE'S LABOR'S
LOST;* Venus and Adonis pub-
lished.
Death of Marlowe.
Theaters closed on account of
plague.

1594
Shakespeare's T W O GENTLE-
MEN OF VERONA;* The Rape
of Lucrece published.
Shakespeare's company becomes
Lord Chamberlain's Men.
Death of Kyd.

1595
The Swan theater built.
Sidney's *Defense of Poesy* pub-
lished.
Shakespeare's ROMEO AND JU-
LIET,* A MIDSUMMER
NIGHT'S DREAM,* RICHARD
II.*
Raleigh's first e x p e d i t i o n to
Guiana.

1596
Spenser's *Faerie Queene* (Books
IV–VI) published.
Shakespeare's MERCHANT OF
VENICE,* KING JOHN.*
James Shirley born.

APPENDIX

1597
Bacon's *Essays* (first edition).
Shakespeare's *HENRY IV*, Part I.*

The Wisdom of Solomon Paraphrased (poem). First published verse.

1598
Demolition of The Theatre.
Shakespeare's *MUCH ADO ABOUT NOTHING,* *HENRY IV*, Part II.*
Jonson's *EVERY MAN IN HIS HUMOR* (first version).
Seven books of Chapman's translation of Homer's *Iliad* published.

Matriculated at Queen's College, Oxford, 9 April.

1599
The Paul's Boys reopen their theater.
The Globe theater opened.
Shakespeare's *AS YOU LIKE IT,* *HENRY V, JULIUS CAESAR.*
Marston's *ANTONIO AND MELLIDA,* Parts I and II.
Dekker's *THE SHOEMAKERS' HOLIDAY.*
Death of Spenser.

Micro-Cynicon: Six Snarling Satires (poems) published.

1600
Shakespeare's *TWELFTH NIGHT.*
The Fortune theater built by Alleyn.
The Children of the Chapel begin to play at the Blackfriars.

The Ghost of Lucrece (poem).

1601
Shakespeare's *HAMLET,* *MERRY WIVES OF WINDSOR.*
Insurrection and execution of the Earl of Essex.
Jonson's *POETASTER.*

1602
Shakespeare's *TROILUS AND CRESSIDA.*

Married to Mary, or Magdalen, Marbeck.*
CAESAR'S FALL, with Dekker, Drayton, Munday, Webster (lost,

Admiral's Men); *THE CHESTER
TRAGEDY, OR RANDALL
EARL OF CHESTER* (lost, Admiral's Men); *THE FAMILY OF
LOVE** (Admiral's [?]).
BLURT MASTER CONSTABLE
(Paul's Boys).
14 December, receives five shillings
for a prologue and epilogue for a
court performance of *FRIAR BACON AND FRIAR BUNGAY.*

1603
Death of Queen Elizabeth I; accession of James VI of Scotland
as James I.
Florio's translation of Montaigne's
Essays published.
Shakespeare's *ALL'S WELL THAT
ENDS WELL.**
Heywood's *A WOMAN KILLED
WITH KINDNESS.*
Marston's *THE MALCONTENT.**
Shakespeare's company becomes
the King's Men.

*THE PHOENIX** (Paul's Boys).
*The True Narration of the Entertainment of His Royal Majesty
from Edinburgh till London*
(pamphlet).

1604
Shakespeare's *MEASURE FOR
MEASURE,** *OTHELLO.**
Marston's *THE FAWN.**
Chapman's *BUSSY D'AMBOIS.**

Son Edward born.*
*The Ant and the Nightingale, or
Father Hubburd's Tales;* and *The
Black Book* (pamphlets).
THE HONEST WHORE, Part I,
with Dekker (Prince Henry's Men);
THE PURITAN, OR THE WIDOW OF WATLING STREET (?)*
(Paul's Boys).

1605
Shakespeare's *KING LEAR.**
Marston's *THE DUTCH COURTESAN.**
Bacon's *Advancement of Learning* published.
The Gunpowder Plot.

*MICHAELMAS TERM; A MAD
WORLD, MY MASTERS; A
TRICK TO CATCH THE OLD
ONE* (all acted by Paul's Boys).

1606

Shakespeare's *MACBETH*.*
Jonson's *VOLPONE*.*
Tourneur's *REVENGER'S TRAG-EDY*.*
The Red Bull theater built.
Death of John Lyly.

THE VIPER AND HER BROOD (lost).

1607

Shakespeare's *ANTONY AND CLEOPATRA*.*
Beaumont's *KNIGHT OF THE BURNING PESTLE*.*
Settlement of Jamestown, Virginia.

*YOUR FIVE GALLANTS** (Children of the Chapel).

1608

Shakespeare's *CORIOLANUS*,* *TIMON OF ATHENS*,* *PERICLES*.*
Chapman's *CONSPIRACY AND TRAGEDY OF CHARLES, DUKE OF BYRON*.*
Richard Burbage leases Blackfriars Theatre for King's company.
John Milton born.

THE ROARING GIRL,* with Dekker (Prince Henry's Men).

1609

Shakespeare's *CYMBELINE;** *Sonnets* published.
Jonson's *EPICOENE*.
Dekker's *Gull's Hornbook* published.

Sir Robert Sherley's Entertainment in Cracovia (pamphlet).

1610

Jonson's *ALCHEMIST*.
Chapman's *REVENGE OF BUSSY D'AMBOIS*.*
Richard Crashaw born.

1611

Authorized (King James) Version of the Bible published.
Shakespeare's *THE WINTER'S TALE*,* *THE TEMPEST*.*
Beaumont and Fletcher's *A KING AND NO KING*.
Tourneur's *ATHEIST'S TRAG-*

THE SECOND MAIDEN'S TRAGEDY(?) (King's Men); *A CHASTE MAID IN CHEAPSIDE** (Lady Elizabeth's Men); *WIT AT SEVERAL WEAPONS*, (?)* with Rowley (unknown company).

*EDY.**
Chapman's translation of *Iliad* completed.

NO WIT, NO HELP LIKE A WOMAN'S (Lady Elizabeth's Men[?]).

1612
Webster's *THE WHITE DEVIL.**

1613
The Globe theater burned.
Shakespeare's *HENRY VIII* (with Fletcher).
Webster's *THE DUCHESS OF MALFI.**
Sir Thomas Overbury murdered.

NEW RIVER ENTERTAIN-MENT 29 September (civic entertainment); *THE TRIUMPHS OF TRUTH,* 29 October (civic pageant), for the installation of Sir Thomas Middleton as Lord Mayor of London.

1614
The Globe theater rebuilt.
The Hope theatre built.
Jonson's *BARTHOLOMEW FAIR.*

THE MASQUE OF CUPID (lost, Merchant Tailors Hall).

1615

*THE WITCH** (King's Men); *MORE DISSEMBLERS BESIDES WOMEN** (King's Men).

1616
Publication of Folio edition of Jonson's *Works.*
Chapman's *Whole Works of Homer.*
Death of Shakespeare.
Death of Beaumont.

THE WIDOW(?)** (King's Men); *HENGIST, KING OF KENT** (King's Men); *THE NICE VA-LOR*(?)** with Fletcher (King's Men).
CIVITATIS AMOR (civic pageant).

1617

THE TRIUMPHS OF HONOR AND INDUSTRY (civic pageant).
A FAIR QUARREL, with Rowley (Prince Charles's Men).

1618
Outbreak of Thirty Years War.
Execution of Raleigh.

*THE OLD LAW,** with Rowley and Massinger (King's Men[?]).
The Peacemaker (pamphlet).

1619

THE INNER TEMPLE MASQUE, OR MASQUE OF HEROES; THE

WORLD TOSSED AT TENNIS,
with Rowley (both Prince Charles's
Men).
*THE TRIUMPHS OF LOVE AND
ANTIQUITY,* 29 October (civic
pageant).
On the Death of Richard Burbage
(elegy).

1620

Settlement of Plymouth, Massachusetts.

Appointed City Chronologer, September 6.
*The Marriage of the Old and New
Testament*(?) (pamphlet).

1621

Robert Burton's *Anatomy of
Melancholy* published.
Andrew Marvell born.

*ANYTHING FOR A QUIET
LIFE,* with Webster (?) (King's
Men); *WOMEN BEWARE WOMEN* (King's Men [?]).
THE SUN IN ARIES, with Munday (?) (civic pageant); *HONORABLE ENTERTAINMENTS* (civic entertainments).

1622

Henry Vaughan born.

THE CHANGELING, with Rowley (Lady Elizabeth's Men).
*AN INVENTION FOR THE
LORD MAYOR* (private entertainment); *THE TRIUMPHS OF
HONOR AND VIRTUE* (civic
pageant).

1623

Publication of Folio edition of
Shakespeare's *COMEDIES, HISTORIES, AND TRAGEDIES.*

THE SPANISH GYPSY, with
Rowley (?) (Lady Elizabeth's
Men). *THE TRIUMPHS OF INTEGRITY* (civic pageant).

1624

A GAME AT CHESS (King's
Men).

1625

Death of King James I; accession
of Charles I.
Death of Fletcher.

1626
Death of Tourneur.
Death of Bacon.

1627

1628
Ford's *THE LOVER'S MELAN-CHOLY.*
Petition of Right.
Buckingham assassinated.

1631
Shirley's *THE TRAITOR.*
Death of Donne.
John Dryden born.

1632
Massinger's *THE CITY MAD-AM.**

1633
Donne's *Poems* published.
Death of George Herbert.

1634
Death of Chapman, Marston, Webster.*
Publication of *THE TWO NO-BLE KINSMEN,* with title-page attribution to Shakespeare and Fletcher.
Milton's *Comus.*

1635
Sir Thomas Browne's *Religio Medici.*

1637
Death of Jonson.

1639
First Bishops' War.
Death of Carew.*

1640
Short Parliament.
Long Parliament impeaches Laud.
Death of Massinger, Burton.

THE TRIUMPHS OF HEALTH AND PROSPERITY (civic pageant).

Death of Middleton. Buried 4 July at Newington Butts.

1641
Irish rebel.
Death of Heywood.

1642
Charles I leaves London; Civil
War breaks out.
Shirley's *COURT SECRET*.
All theaters closed by Act of Parliament.

1643
Parliament swears to the Solemn
League and Covenant.

1645
Ordinance for New Model Army
enacted.

1646
End of First Civil War.

1647
Army occupies London.
Charles I forms alliance with
Scots.
Publication of Folio edition of
Beaumont and Fletcher's *COMEDIES AND TRAGEDIES*.

1648
Second Civil War.

1649
Execution of Charles I.

1650
Jeremy Collier born.

1651
Hobbes' *Leviathan* published.

1652
First Dutch War begins (ended
1654).
Thomas Otway born.

1653
Nathaniel Lee born.*

1656
D'Avenant's *THE SIEGE OF*

RHODES performed at Rutland House.

1657
John Dennis born.

NO WIT, NO HELP LIKE A WOMAN'S published.

1658
Death of Oliver Cromwell.
D'Avenant's *THE CRUELTY OF THE SPANIARDS IN PERU* performed at the Cockpit.

1660
Restoration of Charles II.
Theatrical patents granted to Thomas Killigrew and Sir William D'Avenant, authorizing them to form, respectively, the King's and the Duke of York's Companies.

1661
Cowley's *THE CUTTER OF COLEMAN STREET.*
D'Avenant's *THE SIEGE OF RHODES* (expanded to two parts).

1662
Charter granted to the Royal Society.

1663
Dryden's *THE WILD GALLANT.*
Tuke's *THE ADVENTURES OF FIVE HOURS.*

1664
Sir John Vanbrugh born.
Dryden's *THE RIVAL LADIES.*
Dryden and Howard's *THE INDIAN QUEEN.*
Etherege's *THE COMICAL REVENGE.*

1665
Second Dutch War begins (ended 1667).
Great Plague.

Dryden's *THE INDIAN EM-
PEROR.*
Orrery's *MUSTAPHA.*

1666
Fire of London.
Death of James Shirley.